BEAN RE

MOTORCYCLE NOMAD

✪ ✪ ✪

Timothy Remus

Published by:
Wolfgang Publications Inc.
P.O. Box 223
Stillwater, MN 55082
www.wolfpub.com

LEGALS

First published in 2012 by Wolfgang Publications Inc., P.O. Box 223, Stillwater MN 55082

ISBN 13: 978-1-935828-70-9

Printed and bound in U.S.A.

COVER IMAGE

The "Western Novel" cover of Bean're as train robber is the work of David Uhl, well-known painter of various period-correct Harley-Davidson and motorcycle images. You can find the full portfolio of David's work, as well as limited edition prints of this image, at:
www.uhlstudios.com

BACK COVER IMAGE

The back cover image of Bean're with signature top hat and the Buffalo Chip as back-drop, is just one more amazing photo from the man known for thousands of amazing motorcycle images - Michael Lichter. The full range of Michael's work can be viewed and purchased on line at:
www.lichterphoto.com

BEAN'RE
MOTORCYCLE NOMAD

✪ ✪ ✪

ACKNOWLEDGMENTS

✪ ✪ ✪

The Acknowledgments are always the last thing I write. Which means it's almost time to ship this book to the printer. Which also means it's been four or five weeks of working extra hours in hopes of actually having some of these to sell in Sturgis.

I have to start with Bean're. I don't know what he puts on his Cheerios in the morning, but the boy does have a lot of energy. Whenever I call he's there. When I ask for something he gets it. He never gets cranky, and never says: no, I can't.

I think maybe the best chapter in this book is Chapter Seven, Friends. It would not be the same book without all those heart-felt comments and stories. Thanks to one and all for taking the time to send those along. Among Bean're's many friends is a woman by the name of Nerisse Trombetta. Author of the very well-written Chapter Nine, Nerisse also contributed most of pictures we used of both Europe and Australia.

At the very beginning, Bean're and I agreed the book needed photos, lots of photos. So I planned three, 16 page photo sections. Might not sound like a lot of pages to fill, but it was and is. Some of the photos are mine, some we borrowed from Bean're's Facebook page (sorry if we used your photo without giving you any credit), but the best ones came from Michael Lichter and Jack Mcintyre (both have excellent web sites). Thanks to both for the help filling those 48 pages.

The cover image isn't a picture of course, it is instead a very nice piece of art created by David Uhl, thanks David.

No matter how many times I read one of our books, I never catch all the typos and mistakes. Thus comes the need for my crack team of proof readers, Mikey Urseth and Bill Koch. Both are long time riders, and both left Bean're's "voice" very much intact.

Last, but not least, thanks to Jacki Mitchell, my art director and graphics wizard. This is the woman who figured out which photo to put where and how to stitch together what is for us an unusual package of type and photos.

Timothy Remus

FROM THE PUBLISHER

✪ ✪ ✪

I met Bean're for the first time a few years ago at the annual Cincinnati V-Twin Trade Show. Since then our paths have crossed again and again, and along the way we somehow came up with the idea of doing a Bean're Book (I sometimes call it the Book of Bean're).

Writing and publishing a book is nothing new for me, I've been writing and publishing books for longer than I care to admit. What is different is the nature of this particular book. I'm a motorhead and most of the books I've written and/or published show the reader How To Build a Cheap Chopper, Build a Hot Rod Chassis or Airbrush a Bitchin' set of Flames. In short, I would rather write about carburetors and than the party at the bar or the turnout at the rally.

So here I am doing what is essentially a biography. The ultimate life-style book - about a guy who looks like a drug fiend and turns out to be not only sober, but gentle and charming as well.

I just finished reading the entire Friends chapter, the long and short submissions from some of Bean're's best-known fans. I have to say I'm impressed. The one thing that comes through in all of them is the fact that Bean're is who he is. He is true to this unusual path he's chosen to follow. It's not a contrived act. It is simply Bean're. Very few people could pull this off - the signature top hat or purple pimp suit - without looking like a fool, or worse. He can do it, all of it, because his faith in himself and what he does is rock solid.

I could explain that I agreed to do this book because I wanted to try a new marketing niche. Or because I thought Bean're's many fans would guarantee good book sales. And those reasons are certainly part of the reason. But at the end of the day the reason I agreed to assemble and publish this book is the same reason all those people in Chapter Seven sent in their letters and emails – because once you get to know him, it's really hard to not like The Bean're.

Timothy Remus

ONE

PRE-BEAN'RE

As a little kid I remember when my mom and dad got divorced, I was around five or six, and I went back and forth from one to the other. I lived with my mom for a while, and then I lived with my father. Eventually, my mom got remarried and I moved in with her and my stepfather, who later adopted me. I remember early on, when my sister and I were living with my mother, how poor we were. We didn't have any money at all. It's a miracle we even made it. One of the things I remember is walking up the street, I couldn't have been more than about five years old and I was arguing with my mother. I wanted to do some stuff and she said no, we couldn't do it because we didn't have the money - that was always her excuse for not doing something. I remember telling my mother, "When I get older, I'm going to show you, I'm going to do stuff without any money."

And it's kinda strange that I remember that. Why did I remember it? Apparently it had a big impact on me at the time.

All of this happened in Louisville, Kentucky, where I grew up. I went to Catholic schools there, in fact I was an alter boy. We went to the fish fry every Friday night, and on weekends there was always a picnic for one of the churches. We would all go, the kids would play games and the adults would drink beer. The whole idea was to raise money for the church.

Early on I really liked mechanical objects. I always took things apart to see how they worked. Of course I was young, so according to Mom, I never could get them back together. Then I discovered bicycles. I really liked bicycles. I could and did ride everywhere. In fifth or sixth grade I did my first out-of-state bicycle ride. My friends and I rode through downtown Louisville and crossed the Ohio River Bridge from Kentucky into Indiana. We hung out in Indiana for a while and then rode back home over a railroad trestle that was closed down, that was pretty advanced for young kids. That was fun.

About the same time I started chopping bicycles, learning ways of putting on longer forks and doing stuff like that. In eighth grade I traded some stuff I had for a mini bike. We didn't have any money so if I wanted something like a mini bike I had to wheel and deal and trade things.

The mini bike never had a throttle on it. You had to just reach down and hold the carburetor open with your hand and that's how you made it go. That was my first mini bike and it was a chopper. It had a long front end with a sissy bar, and a little Briggs and Stratton motor. I remember my girl-friend up the street, cute little girl, she was riding with me one time. We were riding up the alley and the oil cap came off the motor while it was running. It sprayed oil out all over the place and totally covered us. I thought that was the coolest thing ever. That sealed my fate - that was it for me. What some people would be bummed-out about, I really dug.

I was still in grade school at this point, but on Friday nights I went to the Football games. And we drank. I had a lot of older friends with cars, so we'd all ride around, it was cool to go cruising. We'd get twelve beers, and go to the park or whatever and everybody else would be doing the same thing. And if the park rangers or police caught ya, they'd just make you pour the beer out and send you home.

Even if you got caught with weed it was the same thing, they'd dump the weed out on the ground and send you home. That was back before you did federal time for possession of a joint, or lose your license for life, because you were drinking and driving.

Eventually, drinking and smoking pot started to take up most of my time. I did a lot of partying. I had part time jobs, and like everybody else I was trying to fit in. Around this same time my father died, my real father. I didn't have any contact with him, but because he was my natural father, it meant I could receive Social Security funds to go to college.

My sister is four years older than me, she was 18 when he died so she went to college and became a registered nurse. When it got closer to my graduation I realized that the whole college scene probably wasn't for me. I applied to college and was accepted. Like I said, it would've been paid for by Social Security, but instead I opted to go into the Marine Corps. I figured; let's get my life started. I was over school and it was time.

THE MARINES

So I went in the Marine Corp in 1981. The pay then was about $469 a month. When I started getting a couple promotions I think I made it to $550 a month. The whole time I was in I lived in what they called an open squad base, which is one giant room with 60 to 80 people, nothing but bunk beds and wall lockers.

It was different, a very different kind of living. The bathrooms for example, they didn't have walls. There was zero privacy. You had a shower room, and one row of crappers and one row of pissers on the other wall. No sinks in between. People would be sitting on the crapper and you'd be saying "Hey pass me down that magazine" and people would be talking. So you learned to accept a lot of that stuff and it changes your life. It changes the way you look at things. When I got out I realized it really couldn't get much worse; even living on the street might be a little better, in terms of basic comforts, than living on base. Those were some pretty rough times.

During my time in the marines I kept right up with my drinking and smoking. That was right at the time when they were starting to crack down pretty hard on marijuana use. Drug testing was new and they started testing all the time. Well, I smoked a lot of pot and we were told that marijuana stays in your system, in your fat cells, for 30 days. Maybe it was because I was very thin and had very low body fat, but I smoked pot pretty near every day and I never failed a urine test.

The Marine Corps was down on pot smoking, but drinking was fine. You could close the bar at 2:00 in the morning and stay out all night. As long as you were back when the squad base opened at 5:30 or 6:00 in the morning, everything was OK. There were no problems with that.

I did get in trouble one time on Halloween night. I was in town and I had on a flasher costume. I used my Marine Corp raincoat, but I took the stripes off. With no military markings it technically isn't part of your uniform and that was okay to wear. I took some pants legs and cut them off at the knees and tied them up with shoelaces so they hung out the bottom of the raincoat and it looked like I had pants on. But all I really had on underneath was baby blue bikini underwear, like a Speedo and that was my costume and it looked legit. I even took a shirt and cut the collar off, and had the collar around my neck under the raincoat, because you had to wear a shirt with a collar, even when you were in civilian attire.

People would see me and say, "what's your costume?" and I'd flash them. Well everything was cool; I was bar hopping, you know, always the life of the party. I went to one bar and I picked up a civilian girl, who was dressed as a nun. She was in a habit and she was pretty freaky. The best part of her costume was she had nothing on under the costume. So I had her under one arm and we're off bar hopping and we went down to Court Street, which is closed now. Court Street in Jacksonville, NC was nothing but strip clubs and pawnshops and tattoo shops. It was always trouble.

So this nun and I are walking down the street and there was shore patrol walking the other way. Shore Patrol is military MPs and civilian police officers working together. One of the MPs stopped me and said, "Hey, you don't have a collar on. You got to have a shirt with a collar." and I turned around and I pulled my collar out from under the jacket and they said, "Okay, alright, you can go," and I turned around and as we were walking away one of my pant legs fell down. So the cop tells me to come back and open up my raincoat. I said, "Alright, but you're not going to like this, remember it's Halloween." So I open up my raincoat and they laugh. They laughed hysterically. They thought it was so funny that they got on the radio and called some more MPs to come and I had to open up my raincoat for them. They were all laughing when the officer of the day walked up. He's the one in charge of all the MPs. So I had to show him too, and he wasn't laughing. Immediately none of them were laughing anymore either. Now it was a serious offense.

So they arrested me and they put me in jail. They took me to the city jail first, and then later I went to the brig. While I was in the city jail all the cops came to my cell and said, "Okay open your raincoat." So I did and they thought it was funny as hell. But in the end, I got court marshaled for that. Being in town wearing a raincoat in my underwear. You know it sounds pretty bad, especially when it's out of context.

That was a huge run in. When I got out of the brig they gave me a court-appointed lawyer, who was a second lieutenant, which means he's just come to the military. He's a new officer. He did get me through the process. I had to spend some time in the brig and I lost one of my two stripes, but it could have been worse. When I left his office he told me, "I don't ever want to see you again. You're lucky... stay out of trouble and fly straight like a good Marine."

Well, two weeks after I got out, I was hitchhiking back to base late at night. I was drunk. I was so drunk I was falling down, and in the process I scraped-up my face so I looked a little rough. Anyway, I was stumbling back, trying to hitch-hike and a taxicab full of Marines going back on base picked me up. When we got to the main gate, the MP told the cab driver to pull over to the side. And when they pulled us out of the cab, there was a marijuana pipe on the floor of this cab. So automatically it was mine, bam. And I said nah, I don't know what you're talking about, that's not mine. They were also worried that I might have a concussion, so they took me to the hospital and in the process they drew blood.

This was Friday night, on the following Monday, as soon as our company was back in order, they immediately gave me a urine test and then they charged me with possession.

That's about four charges right there: possession of drug paraphernalia, possession of marijuana (the pipe had resin on it), smoking pot, and attempting to venture onto base with drug paraphernalia. That's enough charges to get you an Article 15, which is conspiracy. Basically if you commit a crime and you knew that crime was against regulations, and you did it anyway, in effect you conspired against the military, which is almost treason.

I watched a lot of people go down with an Article Fifteen, and get ten to fifteen years. If you get more than a year, you usually go to Leavenworth, I had plenty of friends go there. When I go to see the attorney it's the same lawyer that I had the first time and he just flips out. He says, "I can't believe you're back. I told you I never wanted to see you again. It's only been two weeks and here you are again. Whatever you get this time is what you deserve, cause you're a hard head."

Next, he opens up my file and starts reading it and then he says, "It says here that both of your tests came back negative for marijuana, both the blood test and the urine test. How is that possible?" And I look at him and I tell him that I smoke pot every day of my life, "I always have and I always will until I die. If those are your tests, you tell me what's up." Well, he dismissed me and I left and never saw him again. He sent me back to my company, but I was under restriction, I was restricted to the base and couldn't leave. But I kept breaking restriction. I kept going off base and coming back late, and then more charges would pile up against me.

It was ridiculous. Finally, just as I was finishing my third year, exactly to the date, they came up to me with a piece of paper. They offered me a general discharge under other-than-honorable conditions, in lieu of a court marshal. They said, "You sign this and we'll drop all the charges and you can just go. And in six months you can upgrade it to honorable." I said, "That's cool, that's what I want to do." But really, that was all bull; they made me that offer because they didn't have enough to convict me.

So after over two years of perfect duty, with letters of appreciation and meritorious marks, which are like awards that you get for doing good things and absolutely zero bad stuff, things started going downhill during my last year. I did take their offer. When I left in 1984, I wouldn't say I had an attitude, but I did feel like I'd been through hell and life could never get that bad again.

The whole reason I went in the Marine Corp was to buy a motorcycle. I thought I'd have some money and good credit when I got out and be able to buy a brand new Harley-Davidson. When I did get out though I couldn't even afford a used Harley.

So after getting out of the Marines I went back to Kentucky. My sister and my family were worried about me and they wanted me to come home. Once I got there I got kind of stuck in a rut. I worked a couple jobs; my first job when I first got out of the Marines was driving a truck for L Hartman and Sons in Louisville. They sold bulk raw bakery goods - 100-pound bags of flour, cake mixes and such.

When I was off work I hung out with a lot of motorcycle guys, I think I was kind of refining my motorcycle roots. I ended up buying a Triumph, which I kept for many years but it was awhile before I got it running consistently.

LEAVING LOUISVILLE

Of course I was drinking a lot and after two years of living at home I needed a new plan. It was 1986 and I decided to leave Louisville, Kentucky, and hitchhike to Florida. I figured I would go to the boat docks and get a job on a shrimp boat.

I thought that because the boats go out for two weeks at a time I could make a two-week paycheck and come back in and have money to start over. Well I didn't know anybody and I didn't know anything about fishing or shrimping. Shrimp boats don't even go out that long, most of them go out daily, they work long days, but they do come back every day. The fishing boats that go out into deep water, some of those do stay out for a while, but those are northern boats. I know that today, back then I just had all this stuff in my head. I call them Fred Flintstone ideas. I had this plan and I'm going for it. I guess the problem was I didn't have a Barney to rely on.

Anyway, I set the date I was going to leave and as the time got closer, I was determined to leave on that date. It was midsummer and I'd already given two weeks notice to quit my job. I got my last paycheck and it was only about $200. I knew that wasn't enough to start over again, so I went to Churchill Downs. That was my plan, go to the racetrack and bet on some horses. I figured there isn't much difference between two hundred dollars and nothing if you're starting over. Needless to say I left the track with about thirty bucks and so I didn't have enough money and the next day when it came time to leave, I told my stepdad I wasn't leaving that day.

I finally did leave. My stepdad dropped me on the shoulder of the road outside Louisville early on a Saturday morning with my trusty sea bag so I could start hitchhiking to Florida, to start my plan to work on a shrimp boat.

While I was hitchhiking I decided to stop in Camp Lejeune, Jacksonville, North Carolina and see some of my old friends that I hadn't seen in two years. I figured I would spend a couple weeks there and maybe even live there. But I hadn't been there more than a week, maybe even five days, and I just hated it, hated everything about it, I was so over it. All the people I thought were my hardcore friends were pretty much losers. It didn't appeal to me, so I started hitchhiking to Florida again, but as I went down south, I decided to stop and try to find this friend I had in Charleston, South Carolina.

This is how I met this guy. I had just gotten out of the Marine Corp and had a date with an old girlfriend. I picked her up and we decided to go to this little bar where I hung out sometimes. Now it's a very rough, rough bar, but it was during the day, so I thought, what trouble can happen at 3:00 P.M. in the afternoon? So we go to this bar and start drinking draft beers, they're cheap, like 50 cents a mug and that's what we're doing. We both got a second beer and there's no one in the bar except two girls working behind the bar and one guy who I've never seen before all the way down at the end of the bar.

As I'm sitting there talking to her three guys come into the bar and go straight to the end of the bar, surrounded the guy, and start talking crap to him. You know, things like, "We're going to kick your ass, you don't know who we are, and you messed with the wrong person last week," and all this stuff. I didn't know the guy or what was going on but it didn't matter. One of the things they said was something about his bandana, "You think you're some kind of hippie, blah, blah, blah," and at the time I was just starting to grow my hair long and I thought no, that's not right. That's uncalled for.

I looked over at my girl, and said, "You know I'm probably going to regret this," and I turned around and I said, "Is there a problem down there?" Well immediately the three guys come down to get me, so as they were coming, I'm getting off my barstool, but I wasn't quick enough. One had already picked up a pool stick and poked me in the chest with it, told me to sit back down, so I sit back down and he's yelling and swinging this pool stick around and ranting. I'm thinking, okay, this is what I gotta do. I'm going to take a big drink of this beer and pretend not to look around and then I'm gonna hit him with the mug. So I take a big drink, and as I'm taking a big drink, he swung the pool cue and he stopped it an inch from my face. I had my eyes closed; I was drinking a beer, getting ready to execute my plan. Well, because I didn't flinch or move or anything, it freaked him out and he thought, this dude is crazy. This dude is gonna kill us all. So he talked some more shit, but he changed his tune immediately and when he was done he said, "That's it, we're going to leave and you're just lucky that we don't kick your ass," then all three of them left. The girl looked at me and goes, "Wow, you could have taken those three guys, I'm impressed."

So yeah, it was awesome; I became good friends with Jeff, the guy at the end of that bar. So on the way south I decided to stop in Charleston and see him. I had his phone number and an address, but I didn't call that number until I got to Charleston. I found the address before I called, it was a nice apartment complex, not what you would think. Of course, nobody's home because this is during working hours.

THE MOVE TO CHARLESTON

So I went down to the end of the street, turned and walked until I found this little bar called the Ram Room. Turns out it's a redneck bar for blue-collar workers, mostly roofers and house framers. There was a lot of building going on. Well I went in there and I starting drinking beers, pitchers of beers and there was a girl working the bar and she's like "Wow, you're hitchhiking, that's your stuff? Well you know if you can't find your friends, you're welcome to stay in the back of the bar." And as the day progressed more and more workers started showing up. I told one of the roofers that I had done some roofing in Kentucky, so I knew a little bit about it. Well he offered me a job, "Show up Monday morning if you want the job. We'll pick ya up." So I thought well, that's cool. That's an option.

Later that night I got ahold of Jeff. I'm like; "Dude, what are you doing?" And he's, "Where are you?" I'm like, "I'm right down the street." So he says to come on over. I walked back to his house and right away I meet his roommate Dave, and we ended up becoming really good friends. They said, "Hey, it's a two-bedroom place, you can stay here in the dining room, and we can split the rent three ways." They even gave me one week with no rent, so I could make some money. That was very cool. So I ended up staying in Charleston, South Carolina for a long time. I got there in 1986 and I moved away in 1991.

When I got to Charleston I was really partying hard, drinking and doing every kind of drug imaginable. I'd always had my own rules about what I would and wouldn't do, in terms of drugs. About that time I started breaking a few of those. One of the things I said I'd never do was needles, I definitely broke that one.

That's when I started worrying that maybe I had a problem. One of the problems I had was quitting for short periods. I would quit drinking and doing drugs for a week and then when I did go back, I'd drink my usual amount and I didn't have the tolerance to hold it.

TAKING THE PLEDGE

It was in 1988 when I decided I'd quit for good, and it's another interesting story. I was partying with this girl, Maraia, she had a job renovating apartments when people moved out. She would go in and do a quick paint job, clean everything up, add a couple of little knickknacks and earn 250 dollars. I started working with her and we'd split the money. But I told her right off the bat, the only way I'd work for her is if she had some weed. I wasn't going to paint an apartment unless I got high. So she always had weed. Along the way she changed though, she got clean and sober. All of a sudden she was giving me these brochures: What an addict is, who is an addict, and all this stuff.

Well I looked at the pamphlets she gave me and I'm trying to figure it out. One of the brochures had 15 questions, and if you answered yes to so many of them then you had a problem. I pretty much answered yes to every single one of them. So I knew, everyone else had known it for a while. Like most people though I was the last one to admit it.

What was funny is that I still had my Triumph at that time, it still wasn't running, but I had the bike. One of my friends had a Triumph-powered trike that he rode for many years. He had always been a diehard Triumph fan, but one day he decided to go buy a Harley and all of a sudden he wanted nothing to do with Triumphs. He called me up and he said, "Hey, I've got all these Triumph parts, spare motors and lots of other parts. I know you like Triumphs, you come get the stuff and it's yours, but you gotta come get it today."

Of course I didn't have wheels, nothing. I'm like, oh shit what am I going to do? So I walked down to the end of the street and ran into the girl Maraia that I was painting apartments with at night. I see her driving by and I waved her down. She's driving a pickup truck, which was not her typical ride, and I'm thinking, this is perfect. I explained to her, "I need a ride." She goes," I can't, I gotta go to Summerville." "Son of a bitch," I say, "that's where I'm going." She looked at me with those big eyes and got all scared. She goes, "No, no, no, you absolutely cannot come with me." I'm like, "Why not? What's it to you?" She goes. "I'm going to my clean and sober motorcycle club meeting. You know, they're the ones helping me stay clean. You're not welcome there at all, they don't want people like you."

All my life, if I meet you, and you don't like me, that makes it more of an attraction. When people are rude to me I'm like, yeah, alright, you know, we'll see. And I try harder.

So I talked her into letting me tagalong and she's said, "Well let's go get your parts first. Then we can go to my club meeting." We loaded up the Triumph parts, no problem, and headed for her meeting. When we pulled up to the house there are a bunch of people in the front yard, most of the guys are wearing motorcycle colors. They're all grouped around a Sportster and they're pulling off the front cylinder. And I thought that was cool, these guys aren't anything like I pictured. They're actually working on a motorcycle and not just working on it, they're doing major engine work in the front yard. I mean that was right up my alley.

So I got out of the truck and they all turned their heads and gave me some really nasty looks, like who is this guy and why is he here and we don't want his kind. And I thought that was OK. A little later they loosened up a little bit and gave me the rundown on what the club was all about and what it took to become a member.

TWO

CLEAN AND SOBER

I'm at the meeting, and this is how they explained it to me: "First of all you have to be clean and sober. Once you declare your desire to join, we mark your hang around time, that's 30 days, and you got to stay clean and sober those 30 days." Well, I expressed interest. I said, "Maybe I would like to quit drinking. I have tried quitting on my own, but never did anything formally." And they said, "Well, if you quit today, we could talk about it at the meeting, and you can start your hang around time today. After 30 days if you stay clean, you can prospect for us for six months."

So I thought, you know, I'll try this. And they had a NA meeting – Narcotic Anonymous - and I picked up a white chip. As soon as the meeting was over, they had a motorcycle club meeting and then I marked my hang around time. Well that was September 18th, 1988 and I've been clean and sober ever since. I did prospect for them and I became a full riding member. So it's pretty strange how all that happened.

I was in the club for three years - the name of the club was Phoenix MC. Eventually I became vice president of my chapter in Charleston. This was all a really, really happy time for me. It was the combination of being in the club and being clean and sober. It allowed me to get the Triumph running and do the riding that I'd always wanted to do.

The Triumph was cool. It had a 650cc motor set in a rigid frame with a springer front end, coffin tank, and a nice paint job. A year later I bought a Harley Davidson. My first Harley, 1980 FX Wide Glide. Of course, I rebuilt it. The finished bike wasn't real pretty, but it was fairly sound and that's the bike I rode it to Sturgis the first time. That was my goal: to have a motorcycle to ride and make a cross-country trip.

My first trip to Sturgis came in 1990, it was the 50th anniversary of Sturgis when half a million people showed up. It was like Woodstock. I mean really, there weren't enough cops. It was just insanity. There were people everywhere doing all kinds of things. I'd never been there before so I don't know this is not the way it is; I just think this is the way it's supposed to be.

I loved Sturgis. I had a great time, and I've been back almost every year since. This all happened because I was clean and sober. Everything I'm doing today, I couldn't do without being clean and sober.

In fact, those are the reasons that I went in the Marine Corp, to get a Harley, and ride the bike to rallies. I wanted to be a biker you know. All the stuff I read in Easyriders magazine about what a biker was supposed to do, that's what I thought made a biker. The stories about taking a hand full of reds and going into a bar and punching everybody out. I even believed the T-shirt – Ride a Bike, Go to Prison. Eventually I thought, maybe I don't have to do this stuff. Once I stopped my drinking and drugging, then I did more than the majority of people do for sure. I started doing all the things I wanted to do – attending Sturgis and riding to all the places I'd wanted to go. So it worked out real good.

THE ACCIDENT

I was supposed to meet another club brother on the way to Sturgis, because everyone was worried about me. Three months before Sturgis I'd been in the worst accident of my life. A car turned left in front of me and I didn't have enough time to do anything. I was riding down the street on John's Island, SC, near where I lived, when this woman cut in front of me at the last second and I didn't have a chance to hit the brakes. All I did was take a deep breath and that was it.

I had a girl with me, Pam, and we hit the car head on. The bike embedded itself into the car's grill and I was flying through the air. The first thing I thought was, I'm going to die, this is it. And then I thought, maybe there's going to be a miracle and I'm going to miss somehow and live through this. Witnesses said I flew as high as the telephone wires.

So I'm flying through the air, thinking, all I gotta do now is land. You know, they tell you to tuck and roll and skid and don't move until you come to a complete stop. Well, because of the trajectory of our impact, both us went straight up in the air and then we came straight down.

I landed pretty much on my butt. I was numb from the waist down, so I thought I broke both my legs, but that didn't matter, I was alive. So my next thought was Pam. I was on my back and I looked around and I saw her not far from me, lying on her back looking at me. Her eyes were open. I called out to her and she didn't respond, so I called out louder and then she started getting sick. She started dry heaving and then throwing up; again her eyes were open, but she never said anything. I rolled over on my stomach and I crawled to her. By this time witnesses were starting to collect and pretty soon the ambulance came and took us both to the hospital.

When I got to the hospital it turned out my legs were not broken. One knee was really messed up and I couldn't walk for a while. And when I flew over the dash it ripped my scrotum open so one testicle was hanging out. But all things considered I was pretty lucky.

But Pam was in a coma with a head injury. They operated on her, but it didn't do any good. They put a feeding tube in her stomach, not just to keep her alive, but also to keep her healthier because we all thought she was going to come out of it. She never did come out of the coma though. For about the first year, she would sneeze and yawn and do some other involuntary body movements, but that's all she would do. And with time even that lessened.

That was a tough one. That was really hard. I'd just met the girl, hadn't known her that long. I only met her like three times and so she wasn't a real close friend, but still I felt really bad about it. I was at the hospital two days later. I walked in with my cane. When I met her parents I apologized. I didn't know what to say, but I had to meet them.

They said, "It's alright, we don't hold you responsible." I said "Yeah, well you know she was with me on the back of the bike, so even though it wasn't my fault I feel responsible." It turns out they knew everything about the accident and they did a little bit of research on me and found out that I was a good guy and had been clean and sober and that I wasn't drinking and drugging before the accident. They told me that they were glad that she met me. That she'd had a lot of problems with drugs and alcohol in her life, and that they were glad that she met someone like me and maybe some of it would stick and help her to get over this when she got better and that made me feel real good. But something like that accident sticks with you forever. You never really get over it.

When they put in that feeding tube, they did it to keep her healthier for the day when she came out of the coma. Well basically what that did was allowed them to keep her alive and that's all. I stayed in contact with the family for about 10 years but I've lost track of them since. The last time I checked, she was still in a coma, living in a nursing home on that feeding tube.

The accident happened in May and by August of that year I was able to make the 50th anniversary of Sturgis on the same bike. I rebuilt the bike, the frame wasn't bent, but it was totaled. I was able to put it back together and ride it to Sturgis. I realized then that no matter how high I set the bar, I could achieve my goals. The next goal was to do Australia. At about the same time though I realized it would be cheaper and easier to go to Europe with my bike, especially when I got to looking at the map and realized I could do twelve or fourteen countries in less than a month.

After that first trip to Sturgis I came back to Charleston, that was my base. As time went on I did more and more traveling up and down the east coast. Usually, when I get into something I get into it all the way, during that time I became pretty involved in club politics. I was running to be the vice president of the club nationally. But at the same time I started to realize that the politics took up so much energy I had no time to ride my motorcycle. My involvement in the club helped me stay clean and sober, but I reached a point where I wanted to quit and not have to attend to so many things. You can only go to so many events. I was national delegate; I was a lobbyist for my chapter. I was pretty powerful, at meetings people would withdraw their motion as soon as I raised my hand.

Eventually I did quit the motorcycle club. Now I had so much more free time, it opened a huge door so I could do more riding. After 1990, I tried to make sure I didn't miss any of the big rallies or events I really wanted to attend.

FREEDOM - SELF EMPLOYMENT

My real freedom came when I became self-employed. I'd tried it before and it didn't work, but I wanted to try again, because you have a chance to make more money than you would working for someone else. When Hurricane Hugo hit in September of 1989, I had just started my own company in Charleston. When the storm hit, my good friend, Tim Mc-Coskey, came down to help me out. How he came to be working with me is a funny story.

FLASHBACK.
THE RIDE TO JACKSONVILLE

When I joined the motorcycle club, the guys said, "You can't be in a relationship for one year." But I'd met this girl one night before I got clean and sober, and I really liked her, so I said, "I'm already in one." Eventually we became engaged, life was good until one day when she just ended the relationship.

She left, so I got on my Triumph chopper and said, F-this. I decided to ride north, to Jacksonville, North Carolina and check it out. I hadn't been there for six or seven years. The Triumph ran good until I got up there. I was two blocks from Beatles Bar, where I used to hang, when the bike broke. It was the clutch assembly. I let it cool down and pushed the Triumph the final two blocks to the bar. There was only one bike in a parking lot full of cars and it was an old raggedy RD 400. I parked next to the Yamaha, and I'm standing there looking at my bike when a guy comes out with a pool stick. He walks up next to me and starts talking. I'm thinking, "I've heard that voice before." Without even looking up I could see his tattoos, and I realize it's my buddy Tim McCoskey. He and I were in the Marine Corps together.

Tim grew up from Greenville, North Carolina. When we met in the Marine Corps, he told me that he grew up on Pecan Road. Well, my aunt had lived on Pecan Road and it turned out that he moved into the house that my aunt owned before her suicide. Maybe partly because of that we became good friends. But when you get out of the Marines, your actual discharge papers can come at any time, and then all of a sudden, you're gone. He left when I wasn't at the base and I never got to see him again until I run into him at Beatles.

So on this night he comes walking out with the pool cue and he is just carrying on. About the time I realize who he is, he looks down at me and says, "It's fuckin' bean head." We go back into the bar and he introduces me to his girlfriend, who got pissed because the two of them were supposed to leave and instead he wants to stay and talk with me.

When I left after the weekend we both promised to stay in touch. I told him, "You come down to Charleston, stay at my place and make eight to ten bucks an hour working for me." He said, "Let me talk to my boss first."

Well, Hurricane Hugo hit Charleston right after that in September of 1989. I called Tim right away and said, "Dude I need some help, come on down, I will pay you ten dollars per hour." He put in his two-week notice. I needed him so bad though that I called again and said, "I need you for this weekend." He and a buddy came for the weekend, and eventually he moved down and we worked together for the next couple of years.

HURRICANE HUGO

I had never been through a hurricane before. I heard about all these hurricane parties and really wasn't taking it seriously. I was planning on staying at home and watching it on TV. The rain had already begun in the morning and I was taking an afternoon nap on the couch. About 4:00 P.M. I woke up to hear the TV news announcer say that they were signing off the air and heading to high ground. They also said that if you hadn't left yet, you should stay put. Now I started to take it serious and decided to head to a shelter instead of riding it out in my rental house surrounded by tall pine trees.

I grabbed a rain suit and jumped on my bike and rode it to one shelter, but they were full so I took it to a nearby school-shelter and parked the bike in between some handrails. I tied it in place with tie-down straps to keep it from blowing over.

It was a long and scary night, but by dawn the next day the hurricane was over. Everyone came outside and the destruction was everywhere. No one could get more than a few hundred feet in any direction without being blocked by a downed tree or a power pole. No one except for me because I was on my bike. The handrails protected the bike from the blowing debris and the tie-down straps kept it up right.

I was able to ride the three miles to my house by riding on side walks, front yards and across ditches. My home was spared. There were ten trees down and only one was on the house. All of Charleston was in this same condition. For the next two weeks I worked cutting the city out from under all the downed trees. I rode around on my bike with the chainsaw slung over my back. Not only were there trees in the road, the loss of electricity meant no street signals - this was probably as close to Mad Max as anyone in Charleston will ever see again.

I had no electricity at my house for two weeks. I filled a metal washtub up with water in the yard every morning and by the time I got home at night, it was warm from the sun so I had a nice outdoor bath. When the sun went down I would read by candle light.

Tim did finally come and help me. He didn't have a car, but rode down for the weekend with a guy he worked with and I put them both to work. And when the weekend was over, the other fella left and Tim stayed. The next weekend, the same guy came back and brought all Tim's stuff down with him, so Tim just moved into my house full time and we worked together for the next couple of years.

At first the work in Charleston was all tree cutting, but then gradually we started doing roofs, lots of roofs. Before too long my landlord got me to roof several of his properties. When the roofing work slowed down we started to do more remodeling and general maintenance. I learned a lot about working for myself at this time. I didn't really have a system down pat. I knew, however, that I was unemployable after this. I like to run things my way and although I have worked for others since then, but I always end up going back to being self employed.

Tim and I worked in Charleston for the next two years, but then the work started to fizzle out in part because of all the out of state construction workers who moved to Charleston to pick up the extra Hurricane work.

THE VIRGIN ISLANDS

About the same time I heard about a big refinery job going on in the Virgin Islands. A girlfriend's ex-husband give me a name and phone number. I called and the guy there pretty much said, "You got the job, just come on down. "So, based on the phone call I bought a one-way ticket to the Virgin Islands. I bought the ticket on January first which seemed very fitting as I would be starting a new life on a new year.

I had to borrow some money for the ticket, when I arrived I only had $110 to my name. I didn't know any one there, I had that one connection, the guy I talked to on the phone. As soon as I hit the ground on St. Croix Island in the US Virgins, I went straight to his office to report.

When I got there they handed me an application, and I said, "What is this?" They said, "We will be in contact." I couldn't even get in to talk to the guy who promised me the job over the phone.

I needed a place to stay and some people I met suggested a work camp; this woman had cabins divided up into four-man dorms, it was $100 per week for a bunk bed. When I met her she wanted some money, of course I didn't have any, so I ended up working for her that first week to pay for my room.

By the end of the week I started working for her contractor. When she asked him about me, he said, "He's the best I've ever had." So I thought I could work for her and get paid, instead of just using the labor as barter for my room, but she told me, "I will only pay you seven dollars per hour." I said, "I won't work any more for that," so she said, "then you have to move out, and then where are you going to stay?" I had $120 in my pocket after paying the rent. I said. "Hell, I'll live in the street if I have to, if I get arrested at least I'll have a place to stay."

I packed my stuff in the old sea bag and walked out. I figured the contractor likes me, and he knows I'm getting screwed. I called him and he said I could stay in a house he was working on for a day or two and that's what I did.

Then I got to talking with this kid who moved to St. Croix with his aunt and started a low budget landscaping business. He told me that his aunt had three little houses. One, a geodesic dome, was blown out from the last hurricane. There was a hole in the roof at the very top, and there were no doors on the house. When I got on her property I said, "I will fix it up if I can live there." That worked, everybody was happy and I lived there for seven and a half months.

I did eventually get the job at the Hess refinery. They paid 15 to 17 dollars per hour and I worked for at least ten hours per day, with a minimum of one extra day of overtime each week. All of that amounted to about 600 dollars per week, starting a month after I got to there.

St. Croix was a strange island. The white man was a minority there. The other thing I found out, the natives were not friendly. They call themselves Croixians (pronounced crew-shuns) and they're racially opposed to everyone except themselves. They didn't even like the black people from St. Thomas, they had some nasty racial slurs for them.

From the very beginning I saw lots of people get beat up and robbed. All the locals carried guns, but if anyone else was caught with a gun they received one year in jail.

Thugs would come into a restaurant in hooded sweats, and walk out five minutes later. It would always turn out that they had just robbed some guy in the bathroom. No one ever solved any of those crimes, the only crimes that were solved were crimes done by one local against another local. When I see something wrong I stand up for what I believe. I stand up for the little guy or whatever, like way back in that bar room fight. So I knew there would be problems, and I did have run-ins with the locals.

When my job at the refinery started they put me on the night shift. There were only 250 people working at night and we had good access to everything. Once I got hired, they took me to the yard where all the machinery was stored and told me I could drive anything in that yard. Anyone who needed a piece of equipment from that yard would come and get me. I would go get the equipment, do the job and bring the equipment back. They made me a foreman, my hat was supposed to be white, all the others were blue. They didn't have a white hat that was big enough though, so I got a blue hat instead - and it saved me later.

I got into it with the people who lived on the island a couple of times. You can say anything to someone, in fact they talk trash all the time, that's how you show how tough you are. But, you can't have any body contact at all, you can wave your hands, but you cannot touch. The first time they got in my face I smacked the guy's hand away. I never hit him. I got reprimanded for that because I touched somebody.

After that little scrap, they told me, "We will get you." Pretty soon I got into it again with someone else, I grabbed him by the throat. Two friends grabbed me and pulled me back. Again, they told me, "We will get you." He wouldn't fight. He kept talking trash. I knew I was getting close.

Normally, when I got to work at the start of the night shift there would be 3500 people coming out. One day I showed up and no one was coming out - they knew something was going to go down. So I stuck around, I'd never seen a riot before.

A guy in a white hat drove up through the main gate and 200 people surrounded the truck, drug him out, beat the shit out of him and ran back to the parking lot. When another guy tried to go up and drag the body back and they beat the shit out of him too.

So I'm walking out of there to get away from the plant, and a pickup truck filled with locals pulls up beside me. Two young boys were driving, there had to be 20 people in the truck. The driver says, "You want some too." Then they called me names, and drove off. I realized how close I was to getting killed, I threw my hat in the weeds and got out of there. That was a learning experience. It felt like what it must have felt like to be black in Mississippi in the 1950s, I learned there is a time when you can stand up for what you believe in, and a time you can't. I got a plane ticket the next day, but there was a three-day wait to leave the island. In the meantime they shut down the plant until things calmed down.

ANOTHER HURRICANE

When I left for the Virgins Tim kept the house we were staying in and ran the jobs. Even before I went to St. Croix he would sometimes do the bigger jobs without me. Which was OK because I was burning out and wanted more highway time.

When I left St. Croix I headed back to Charleston. I had good friends there, and some money in my pocket, it was good to be back. I didn't rent a place right away. Basically, that was my first experience with couch surfing.

It wasn't too long after I got settled into Charleston that Hurricane Andrew hit Miami. I got there the next day, and that same day I called Tim and told him, "You need to come down here now."

He came down with a van, but we didn't have money for things like plastic tarps and a good chainsaw. We needed a thousand dollars right now, so I went to a bike shop in Charleston. Blue was a member at the shop. I said to Blue, "I need to borrow some money, I need a thousand dollars for two weeks. And I will pay you back fifteen hundred." I gave him title to the bike, he said, "I want the bike too," so I brought in the bike.

Now that we had money, Tim and I bought all these plastic tarps and rope, a chainsaw, and mattresses for the back of the van. Because of my experience in Charleston, I had a pretty good idea exactly what we needed for Miami.

We charged people a hundred and twenty five dollars to cover one half of a roof. A lot of times only one side was hurt badly. As soon as we started doing a house, all the neighbors would come over wanting us to help with their houses. We never left a block until we'd taken care of anyone who needed help. We did a great service. We took checks from people we didn't know and never got stuck with a bad one.

One of the things that happened, everyone is trying to clean up their houses and there were these big trash piles in front of each house. One had these twisted aluminum I-beams lying there that had supported the screening around the swimming pool. Well, some guy driving along stopped and started loading up these twisted aluminum I-beams into his truck. All of a sudden the owner of the house was out there waving a gun around. It was kind of like the wild west in Miami after the hurricane.

We lived in the van for two weeks; finally I said, "let's get out of here." We cashed all those checks, and divided up the money. I had over $3000 in cash when I left the van. I planned to hitch back to Charleston, but I didn't want to be on the road with all that money, so I put $250 in one boot, and took 3000 in one-hundred dollar bills and rolled them up in my bandana.

As soon as I got to Charleston I went to see Blue at the motorcycle shop, paid him back and got on my bike and drove away, that felt good, it was an honor thing. Once I had the bike, I rode back to Miami and went back to work with Tim.

THREE

FIRST-TIME HOMEOWNER

When I got back to work in Miami there was a lot of stress, which comes with running any kind of business. My friend Tim was working with me, and pretty soon he started picking up the jobs by himself. And I decided, you know what, I'd rather work for him and let him handle all the planning, scheduling, invoicing and all the rest.

That way I could work and make a few dollars and skip out when I needed a break, and let him keep working and keep trying to make ends meet. I could be gone for a week or three, until he had more work for me.

When I first came back with my motorcycle, I didn't have a place to stay, so I was staying at a place where a lot of the other bikers were staying. It was called the Blarney Stone Tavern and there was probably, I want to say, at least 20 or 30 people that lived in the parking lot of this bar. The bar itself was totally blown out from the hurricane, but there were generators to supply power. It was a real close-knit group of people staying there. I met them when I was in Miami. I fit in real good and we watched out for each other. It was a good place. You wouldn't have to worry to spend the night.

So one of the first nights I was sleeping there, I had my sleeping bag and I like to sleep under the bike so if someone tried to steal the bike they'd wake me. So I'm under there sleeping and someone woke me up. I look up and there's a shotgun in my face and I'm like, "What the hell are you doing?" And he goes, "Who are you? What are you doing here?" I'm like, "I'm here sleeping." We get in this big rigmarole, 'cause he thinks I'm new there. I actually had been staying there maybe a week. Well he knew everybody there, but he had not been there for that week when I came in. So the argument ended and I finally went back to sleep. I thought we had it settled, but a couple hours later, the same guy woke me up with the shotgun again, wanted to know exactly who I was and what I was doing there. That was pretty interesting to say the least. I mean that's what happens when you hangout at bars, you're going to get some of these people.

FIRST-TIME HOMEOWNER

That's when I realized I needed a place to go. When a friend of mine from Charleston came down to work the hurricane he hauled a little camper trailer with him behind his Toyota pickup truck. One day he asked me if I wanted to buy his trailer. "I'm going back," he said, "I'm done here in Miami and I don't want to tow it, so I'll sell it to you for 500 bucks." It was a tiny little thing; I called it the Yogi Bear camper trailer, because it looked like the ones in the Yogi Bear cartoon.

The trailer was pretty bare inside, just a table that folded-out into a bed, and a super small bathroom. It was tiny little thing. As soon as I bought it I just ripped everything out, built a platform, and dropped on a queen size-mattress. When you opened the door, that's all you saw, just a big bed. Then I hung a TV from the wall and I was officially a homeowner, that trailer was the first home I ever owned. There were some other people there too in the same spot, we were squatting on some property behind a warehouse, we even had power so we could plug in.

They had a port-a-can out in the parking lot so that was the bathroom. I stayed there for two or three months until finally one day we all got an eviction notice. That's when a friend of mine that I'd met at the bar, a biker named J.W., came over and said, "Hey, I heard you need a place to park your camper?" I did, because all I had then was my motorcycle and I couldn't pull a camper with the motorcycle. I told him I needed to be out by New Year's Day. Well, I hadn't seen him for a week or two and I kinda thought that was weird, it was almost the end of December. I figured I had to make another plan. Well, New Year's Day 1993 rolls around and I see his truck come pulling up, and he goes, "Hey, you need to move your trailer, let's go. We'll take ya over to my property." I didn't even know him. He lived out in the woods in Homestead. So he pulled my trailer over there, apologized for not coming sooner, but said he'd been sick with the flu. Once he got the trailer parked he said, "I'm going back to bed," and I didn't see him for another three days.

He and I became really, really good friends over the next 10 years and we remain friends to this day. I was the best man in his wedding. I lived there on that property and then in his house for a long time. We did a lot of stuff together. We always went to Daytona and the rallies together. I learned a lot from him. He wasn't into the vagabond gypsy biker lifestyle. He liked to have a good bike and when he went places, he liked to have a nice room, he didn't mind spending the money. He was in the pool business, building swimming pools, so I helped him do that. He made good money. He was a good entrepreneur. I learned a lot from him. That's where I learned some of my business etiquette. I got used to working hard and then staying in nice places - not a tent. He got married in 1996 and by that time I'd been living in his house for a quite a while.

THE MIAMI HOUSE

When he got married his new wife moved down there and it got a little crowded. It was time for me to move on. It was 1996 and I told him I found a house for sale. This was when all the other houses in Miami were selling for over $100,000. I found one, it was a HUD foreclosed home, and they were asking $55,000. I put a bid in of $48,000, and everyone thought that was too low and I'd never get it. Well it turned out that I did get it. But I needed more money for the down payment. I had $5,000 saved up and I took a personal loan from a friend, because the banks wouldn't loan me money. And I still had to sell my Shovelhead, my first Harley and my only Harley at that point. Then I had enough money to close on the house and move in.

Everyone said they thought that was crazy, that I sold my motorcycle you know? What was I going to do without a motorcycle? And I started telling people that in one year I was going to get a brand new one. At the same time I knew that was probably wishful thinking and it wouldn't happen that quickly.

Well it turns out I got a really good deal on that house, and I believe that was because it was a HUD home. When I saw the open house signs and tried following them to the house, they led me in a big long circle. Actually, they should have just directed people like me directly from the main road to the house. It was almost like they didn't want anyone to find the house.

When I finally did find the house it was back on a dead end street, hidden away from everybody. The realtor was sitting there with her kids at the end of the driveway. When I walked up, she goes, "The house is unlocked, just go around the corner. It's the only one back there. Go in and look, whatever." She wasn't very helpful at all. When I came out, I asked her about it and said, "Could I put a bid in?" She didn't seem to have the time to deal with me. I said, "I have a realtor, I'd like her to contact you," and again she wasn't helpful, didn't want to contact my realtor. And I think in hindsight she didn't want any one to bid on this house. I think she wanted to get the house for herself or her family.

When my realtor told her friends that we were bidding on a HUD home, they said they never ever go for less money than the asking price. And the asking price was already super cheap.

So to get it for $10,000 less than the asking price, that was unheard of. Which meant that the day I moved in I instantly had a big chunk of equity. At the end of my first year in the house I applied for a second mortgage, and a week later the finance company wrote me a check for $22,000. When they gave me the check, I asked them, "Do I need to show you receipts for what I'm doing?" Because I told them I was going to do some home improvements and that's why I wanted the money. And they basically told me no, "That's your money. You can do anything you want." So that was awesome and I immediately went to a Harley dealership and talked to them about buying a motorcycle.

You have to remember though, that was Harley's heyday, there was the list, and you had to wait two years to buy a new Harley. A friend of mine was in-line, so to speak, for over a year and sold his spot on the list for $2,000 just so the person who bought his spot wouldn't have to wait so long to buy a brand new bike. Not only did I not want to wait, but I also wanted a stripped down Road King. I didn't want one with all the bells and whistles. Why pay for all that stuff and then take it all off? It seemed pretty ridiculous, although that was really the only way you could do it then. The dealers were calling the shots and making the rules.

Somebody recommended Doc Hopkins, a dealer from Shawano, Wisconsin. Well, Doc was also a top fuel drag racer. He and I were huge friends, every time he came to Daytona I would pit for his top fuel drag bike. And so I talked to him and I told him I wanted a stripped down police model Road King. Well, he said he was just getting ready to order one for the police in Shawano, and that they were going to lease the motorcycle from him for four months and then it would be his motorcycle to do with what he wanted. So I was like, "Oh, that's perfect. I want that bike." He said, "Well I don't even know how much it's going to be, let me make a phone call and I can find out." The bike turned out to be $12,000 and I said, "It's exactly what I want," and I gave him a deposit and bought him dinner in Daytona.

THE ROAD KING

The police kept the bike all summer, and gave it back to the dealership sometime in September. Before I went up to get it, I called and had the dealership do some work to the bike. I didn't actually pick it up until November of 1997. When I picked it up it had 800 miles on the clock.

When I finally took possession of that new Road King it opened up a whole new world for me. This was a major changing point for me. Up to that point, for most of my life I'd owned motorcycles, but I never could afford a new Harley. In 1988 I bought my first Harley, my Shovelhead, and that's what I rode up to that point. It took every cent that I had to keep it on the road. It was a giant money pit. I rebuilt the bike, the complete bike, at least every two years. Now I actually had a dependable bike I could ride anywhere. My first trip happened right after I bought the bike.

Even though the police used the bike for four months it had never been titled – they leased it from the dealer. When I bought the bike I got a certificate of origin, rather than the title transfer, meaning it was brand new and came with the full one-year warranty. So I was set.

The bike did have one problem. I had the dealership do some motor work to it. I used the dealer to do the work so it would be done right and not hurt the warranty. But during that first year, I had the starter clutch go out six times.

They couldn't figure out why that was happening. You know, that's not supposed to happen. Finally they decided it was a compression issue. But it was weird. Usually, with a really high horsepower, high compression motor, every time you start it, it sounds like a bike with a dead battery. But my bike started like a normal bike. It would turn over fast Rrrr, rrr, rrr, rrr, rrr. Just like it's supposed to. Never a problem. But sometimes, actually somewhat often, while I was turning it over it would stop and sound like a lawn mower that hit a rock and locked up. And that's what was crashing the starter drive.

So I kept taking it back to the dealer. I didn't want that ailment. I wanted the problem fixed so it didn't happen again. I was afraid it was going to keep happening. They pretty much said, whatever, you just have to keep fixing the starter. They were not going to deal with the issue.

I was planning a trip to Alaska, I'd always planned it. I figured that with or without the starter issue, the bike is covered under warranty so I'm thinking this is the perfect time.

I was working a real job at that point, but I quit. That was another one of those times where I just quit. I had to. You know you can only do Alaska in the summer. And because I had a one-year warranty on the bike, I figured I have to do this now. If I don't do it this summer it's going to be a lot harder to do later.

ALASKA TRIP

So the summer rolled, my first summer with this motorcycle. I realized again that this is the best opportunity I'm ever going to have to make the trip. I didn't know if I would get in a relationship and end up settling down. I didn't know if I'll have the money or the time later, or maybe I would be working a full time job, so I said, "I gotta do this." I made the plan and as I came close to the time to leave, I discovered that I didn't have enough money to go. I did have the time though and a new bike with a warranty.

So I came to the realization that there was only one way to do this. I was going to take what money I had and go. When the money ran out, wherever I was I'd deal with it. I rationalized that I have a lot of friends and my friends would do anything for me, just like I would do anything for them.

If they were in a jam, I would bail them out, but I would never lend them money to go on vacation and neither would they lend to me for that reason. So therefore, I figured I'll go on vacation and then when I get in a jam they'll bail me out. That's how I came up with that rationale, and a couple of times it came into play and I got bailed out. When I got back home I got to work and I paid them back. That's how I did that trip.

At about the same time I was getting some tattoo work done from my tattooist, Marty in Melbourne, Florida. I was getting tattooed about a month before I left, I was talking to him about my trip to Alaska and he was real enthused, "Sounds great," he says, "my buddies and I are leaving for the Harley Rendezvous pretty soon." And I said, "Wow, that's awesome, I've always wanted to go to the Rendezvous. You know what, I'm going to go there too, and then from there I'll go to Alaska." He goes, "Dude, do you even know where the Harley Rendezvous is?" I said, "Of course I do." and he goes, "Where?" I said, "It's in upstate New York." He goes, "How do you figure upstate New York's on the way from Miami to Alaska?" I'm like, "Everything is on the way." He didn't believe me. He goes, "We're leaving in a week." I said, "Well, I can leave in about a week and a half, I'll meet ya up there." He was trailering his bike and he had a bunch of people going with him and it was a big deal and I like riding alone, so I'm like, "I'll just meet ya up there, I'm riding."

So I took off from Miami. The bike ran good and so did I. I was young then. I don't even think I was 30. Anyways, I took off and rode pretty much straight through from Miami. Except for gas, I didn't stop for a long, long time. I bet I rode 19 hours, and made it well over 1,200 miles. I still had my starter issue, I think this was probably the third or fourth time I had the starter issue. I kept push-starting the bike. On my way there, I'm going down the highway and I see a Harley-Davidson sign so I pulled up. I told the service guy what was going on and that it was under warranty. I told him I was traveling to Alaska and they were super, super nice. They got the bike in and it was right around 6:00 at night. So they asked one of their mechanics if he'd work late, he said he would. They had me out of there in about an hour and a half, which is fast because it's a big job.

So that worked cool. It didn't slow me down. That was the first time on the trip that the starter went out. I ended up taking off that night from the dealership and I just kept motoring. The next day I arrived in upstate New York for the Harley Rendezvous, but couldn't find my friend's truck. They left two days earlier than I did, but it turned out they blew a water pump on the way and got stuck for two days. Because of that I actually beat them to the Rendezvous.

I stayed there for a week, had a great time and did all the rodeo games. During the rodeo games my starter went out again. The dealer up there was not so nice. I told him I was on vacation. He says, "it's summertime up here. It's been a long winter and everyone wants to ride. Nobody wants to be down." and I'm like, "You don't understand, I'm traveling." It's a difference when you're home and not home. He goes, "I can't bump my local customers for you." Basically, they wanted a week.

When they did bring the bike in to the shop, they noticed first off that the bike already had a lot of miles showing on the odometer. At that time, I had about 15,000 miles on it and it was only six months old. And because I was doing the rodeo games and it rained real hard up there, my bike was covered in mud. It was a white bike, police white; it was so covered in mud you couldn't tell it was white. Every piece on it was covered in mud and I guess they figured I was a guy who abused his bike and didn't really care about it. I wasn't abusing it. I was riding it you know. So that first shop didn't want to work on it. I took it to another shop and they were a little bit more reasonable. I think they got to it three or four days later.

From there I took off for another party, down in North Carolina at JR's. JR was a friend who moved from

Miami up to the North Carolina Mountains and this was his annual party. So I caught the party coming back from New York. After that I rode with some other friends to Atlanta and from there I rode to visit more friends in New Orleans. Before leaving Louisiana I rode all the way north to the top of the state and then come back down and took I-10 all the way to California.

One of the things I wanted to do in California was visit the Redwood Forest. Well I looked at the map wrong. I wanted the Redwood Forest with the giant, really wide trees where you can drive right through. That's not on the coastline though, I ended up at the Land of the Giants. The trees were super, super, super tall, but they're not the wide ones. I made a lot of mistakes like that. Sometimes that's the best though. You plan stuff out, but you also have to be open to the reality of things the way they are. So I headed up the coast on the PCH and went all the way to the border.

BORDER CROSSING INTO CANADA

When I got to the border I stopped and this guy comes over for the inspection. He says, "How ya doing? Where ya going?" I tell him "Alaska." He says, "Where are you from?" then he took my license and asked me the routine questions. "Do you have any fruits and nuts and are you bringing anything into the country that you want to declare. Well the answers were no to all. Then I said, "I do have something to declare," and I had a gut feeling that I might have a problem.

I had, and still have, a concealed weapons permit. It gives me the right to carry a gun and it's good in about 29 states. I thought there might be an issue with the gun, so before I got to the border I unloaded the gun so the shells and the gun were separate. When I told him I had something to declare, he asked what it was. I said, "I have a pistol." "No problem," he says, "just pull over there and we'll inspect it and you can go on about your way."

I pulled over and parked in this special area and before I could get the kickstand down I was surrounded by immigration police and guards and they're all telling me, "Don't move, don't move, where's the gun, freeze, don't move." And I'm like, "Whoa, whoa, whoa." And they're still, "Where's the gun? Keep your hands where we can see them, just tell us where the gun is," and all this. I said, "Look, relax, it's packed away, it's fine." And then they were really on me. I said, "I told you I had one. There's no problem. If there's a problem, I'll leave and go back to the States." "Well there's a big problem," they explained, "and It's too late for that, you're in Canada now."

So they removed me from the bike, and retrieved the gun out of my saddlebag and took it into the office. Then they brought me into an interrogation room. They wanted a bunch more paperwork on my bike and the registration, so I had my wallet out. I'm a friendly guy. I generally like to talk. They asked about my wallet. They go what's that made of? I go, "it's alligator." "Oh okay," and they went about interrogating me. A little while later they asked me about my cowboy boots, and I told them they're stingray. Next they find my hat, which I'm very proud of, so I told them all about it. "It's American rattlesnake with penis bones from a raccoon. It's got porcupine quills and quail feathers.

Finally, after maybe an hour and a half. I said, "Look, I tell ya what. I'll go back to the United States. I'll put the gun in storage till I return, then I'll come back and it's no big deal," 'cause I still didn't think it was that big a deal.

And they said, "Well, that's exactly what we're going to have you do, but we have to admit you into Canada and right now we have a problem because you're bringing endangered species into our country.

I said "Let me tell you about my animals. They've all American. That's American rattlesnake. That's American alligator. None of them are endangered. I bought them legally, there's no problem. The only problem here is that I've got eccentric tastes." And they kinda dropped their heavy attitude, which I don't respond well too. I told them, "Look, I'm going to get rid of this gun, come back, but then do I have to go through all this stuff over again?" And they said, "yes, and not only will you go through it over again here, but you'll go through it again, when you come back to Canada from Alaska.

That's when I said "No I won't. I refuse." And they said, "What do you mean you'll refuse?" I said, "I'm going to take a ferry and I'm going to go around your country. I don't need this from anybody. The only reason I'm riding through now is to keep a schedule because I have a friend and she's flying up to Alaska and I've got five days to go almost 3000 miles to pick her up at the airport." So when I told him that, then they kind of changed their attitude and they finally released me. On the way out of the office, they said, "look, we'll work on your paperwork, when you get back up here we should have your paperwork done. You can come in and get your paperwork and we'll admit you into the country."

So now I had to go back to the United States. I made a U-turn and got into the entry lane for America and the line is backed up for miles. So I'm like, F-this, I ride down the side in between traffic, cut through everybody and I got all the way up to the front of the line and I stopped and waited. Well when they called me forward, I pulled up to the guy and he said where are you coming from? I said, "I'm coming from Alaska." He said, "Do you have anything to declare?" I said, "Absolutely not." And he said welcome to America and I rode through.

The first place I went to was a post-office-box and shipping place. I went in there to see if they had lockers so I could store the gun. The guy was really cool. He said he could hold the gun for me until I came back. He added that I should put my home address on it so if I didn't come back, he would know where to send it. He did that with a nudge-nudge, wink-wink, so I immediately scrapped all plans on returning since I wanted to take a different route back through Canada and into the States anyway.

I did call him when I returned home to ship the gun to me. And it turned into a big deal because he couldn't mail it to a residence. So I had to have him mail it to a gun dealer and that's where I picked it up.

FOUR

CANADA - OH CANADA

Now I'm going to cross back into Canada. I went through the long line, to make sure I got the same person I had before, hoping they would be familiar with my situation, but when I pulled up it was a different person. I guess they switch shifts or whatever. I started explaining my situation and they're like all ready to send me to the special line, and about that time this other person walked up and goes, "Wait, I remember him, he was here earlier. Did you get rid of the gun?" I said "yeah, I got the receipt right here." They didn't even ask to see it. They asked if I got cleared with immigration? And I said, "Oh yeah, all my paperwork's done." They go, "Okay, welcome to Canada."

So I got in. Then a funny thing happened. Canada is a beautiful place. I had no idea. I really thought Canada wasn't worth all the hassle I went through to cross the border. Once you cross the border though, that's when the hassles stop. It's the friendliest country. Since then I've been all over, east, west, I love it up there and the people are great. Once I was over the border I looked at a map. I wanted to get on the ALCAN, but to get on the ALCAN – which runs diagonally northwest from above Montana - I would have to go east and pick it up above Idaho. So I saw a shortcut, a road marked in solid black. On my map, solid black meant it's a highway. A dotted black line meant it's not the best road and could be gravel.

This one was called the Cassiar Highway, it runs straight north and meets up with the ALCAN halfway up into British Columbia. From there I could ride through the Yukon and on to the Alaskan mainland. It was a great plan. I got up to where the highway started and I stopped at a gas station. While I'm pumping gas, there's an RV coming the other way, and it was filthy. It was just covered in this oily brown dirt. When I looked closer I realize it's probably a half million-dollar motor home and I'm thinking, they should wash that thing. But I really didn't think much about it.

I pulled out of the gas station and made it about half a mile and there was this sign: Pavement ends in 500 feet. I thought to myself, I guess they're working on the road or something. Well, no, it was a gravel highway, about 750 miles long. I spent two days on that highway. I ran pretty fast. It was packed gravel and they put oil on the gravel to keep the dust down; there weren't a lot of travelers on it. What I did see was a lot of logging trucks. They would come rolling down in the opposite direction, and even with the oil on the road, they would still kick up a lot of dust. When I met one of those trucks I would wait until I was just about to pass them and duck behind the windshield. Then the bike and I would be pelted with rocks, because they're running 80 miles an hour and I was running every bit of 70 and 80 miles an hour too. It was a packed gravel so you can do that. But needless to say, the bike and I got some huge abuse on that road.

This was in the days before cell phones and I didn't carry a watch. Which meant I had no way of telling time. During that entire trip the sun was my guide. When it got dark, it's time to look for a place to stay, whether it's a campground or a motel.

So I'm running up the Cassiar Highway. I don't have any sort of timetables, don't know what time it is, but the sun is getting low, I'm tired and starting to think it's time to stop for the day. Well, the Cassiar was so desolate and isolated you could literally ride for 100 miles without seeing any civilization whatsoever. That includes a house or a barn or anything. I mean it's wilderness out there.

Finally I see a sign and it says, Cabins Ahead. As I pull in, I'm thinking, I don't know the place looks a little rough. It's a tiny little rural place, there wasn't a town or anything else. Then a woman comes out and she was real nice. I asked her if there were any restaurants, she said no, but she had some soup, and if I was interested she'd give me a bowl of that. I said wow, that's great, yeah. Next, I said, "What about your cabins, what have ya got?" She says, "Well they're just cabins." So I asked her, "Well, do you have TV or cable?" "No, nothing like that."

"Does it have electricity?" She goes, "Yeah, it has a light." "Okay, what about heat?" cause it gets cold up there at night. She goes, "We've got wood burning stoves." I'm thinking yes, "Perfect, perfect." It's this little cabin with a light hanging by the cord from the ceiling. You pull the cord and that's the only electricity in the cabin. I asked her what time it was, because I'm thinking I'm quitting so early. She goes, "It's 11:30." Then I realized I'm getting far enough north that the sun doesn't go down 'till really late.

I fired up the stove, got it cranking, and passed out, about an hour later I woke up sweating. It was probably 200 degrees in that cabin. I stumbled to the door and propped it open and then I went back to sleep. And as I'm going back to sleep, I thought, you know they've got every kind of wildlife imaginable up here, I probably should keep the door shut. But I didn't and everything worked out all right. When I woke up everything was fine. I packed up my stuff and headed out the next morning.

That's when I realized I've got some long days to travel. The sun comes up really early and goes down late. So I just kept rolling and trucked all the way to Anchorage, Alaska.

I made it to Anchorage in plenty of time to pick up my friend Lynn at the airport. She told me ahead of time that if I took her around for a week in Alaska she would help pay for the trip, which was a good plan because I was broke by the time I got to Anchorage.

For one week we rode all around Alaska and did the whole tourist thing. We took a ride in a plane, saw the puffins from a boat, and went to the sea aquarium; we went all over. It was a great week. We did something new every day. One day we rode on a dog sled and on another we went horseback riding. It was a good time. When it was time for me to head back. I dropped Lynn off at the airport and it was almost time for me to start heading south.

Before heading south though I made it the rest of the way to Fairbanks and came back around, so I did the whole loop of Fairbanks and Anchorage before heading south. On the my way back to the 'States I decided to go diagonally southeast all the way down the ALCAN, which took me to Banff' and Lake Louise.

When people ask about the best place I found on that trip, I tell everybody the most scenic place, hands down, was Banff, Lake Louise and Jasper. It's unbelievable. You don't just see wildlife, you see herds of wildlife. You can actually drive down the road and one person can look on one side of the road and the other person can look on the other and you're both amazed non-stop and you're looking at two different things the whole time. Each one of you ends up with a whole different, incredible story to tell later. It's just so much to take in, it's mind-boggling. So I got to see that, that was huge.

STURGIS 1998

When I left the Lake Louise area I headed to Sturgis. Right before I got there my starter went out again and I ended up in a place called Bear Tooth something in Montana. The dealership ran my numbers said I had to call the national office. I'm like, "What? What's the problem?" So I call and they go, "Look, there's a problem here, you keep getting these starters, what are you doing?" I'm like, "What do you mean what I'm doing, I'm starting a bike." They're like, "How do you start it?" I'm like, "What do you mean how do you start? How do you start a bike with electric start? You turn the ignition on and you hit the button." And they go, "Okay, then what happens?" I say, "The motor turns over and then it locks up like a lawn mower hitting a rock." And they go, "what do you do then?" I go, "I let off the button." And they say, "That's your mistake, you should power through it." I go, "Oh I see where this is going. Whatever I do, I've done the wrong thing, I should do the opposite." And we get in this huge argument and the guy starts getting pricky.

He told me they weren't going to honor my warranty for the starter and hung up on me. Of course I didn't have the money to have it fixed and I didn't know what was going to happen. In the meantime, I'm stuck in a motel for two days waiting for them to fix this problem.

Finally he called me back and somewhat apologized. Said he had looked at the charts and that my motorcycle had an S&S carburetor and that voided the warranty. And I said, "What do you mean; you can't have an aftermarket carburetor on it?" He goes, "No, we use Mikuni carburetors sometimes." "So in other words," I said, "one aftermarket carburetor's okay, but the other one isn't and voids the warranty?" He also said there was a problem with the mileage.

At that time, I had 27,000 miles on my motorcycle. He said that was a lot of miles for an eight-month-old bike. I said, "Your warranty is one year unlimited miles, not one year or a lot of miles. So we got in another argument and he hung up again.

Finally he called me back. "Tell ya what we're going to do," he said, "we will honor the parts, but you have to pay the labor this time and we never want to hear from you again." So that was OK, the next time I would have to fix this problem myself, because obviously it was going to happen again.

I make it to Sturgis, this was 1998, and ran into a lot of my friends from Miami. They were all really blown away that I rode my bike from Miami to Sturgis. I'm like, "Dudes, I'm coming back from Alaska." When I got back to Miami the total trip was 17,300 miles and I did it in six weeks with three breakdowns. In upstate New York I was parked for over five days straight. Really, I did the whole trip in five weeks.

As I'm rolling down through Florida, inching closer to home, I started getting really depressed. Then I realized why I was depressed. Because this awesome trip was over. I just told myself I'm going to turnaround and do this all over again really, really soon. I wanted to do it right then, but I couldn't. So I promised myself I really would do it again - and soon.

And that's when it started, on that day. The idea that, first of all, there's no such thing as an idea that's too far out. Second, that I've got a lot of goals and a lot of countries around the world I want to tour on my motorcycle. And all my ideas are achievable one way or another.

Of course I ran out of money on the way home to Florida and had to call my parents so they could bail me out financially. And somewhere along the line I called my friend J.W. too and he wired me a thousand dollars.

Once I explained to these people that I didn't have the money, they didn't question it. No problem. They both said, "How much you need, we'll send you the money. Have a safe trip, glad you're having fun and nothing serious is happening." That's how I did the trip. If I hadn't received that extra money from my family and J.W. when I ran out, I never could have made the trip.

WORKING IN MIAMI

So I learned a lot from that trip and I base my life on it. I started living that kind of life. I got back into Miami and started working. I was working for myself then. I'd work for a week or two, make enough money and then take off and stay gone for as long as that money would last. When the money started running out, I'd start heading back home, get some more work lined up before I got home, so I could make more money and get caught back up on my bills and take off again.

And that's what I did for probably the next seven years. I traveled around a lot up and down the coast. Miami was a good place to live, except that everywhere I went I had to start the trip by going all the way through the state of Florida. That's 400 miles if you go direct north up the coast on I-95 and 500 miles if you go up I-75 towards Atlanta, and it's 810 miles if you go west, across the panhandle and up towards Louisiana. I was going to Daytona every year, and Myrtle Beach and Sturgis. Every time I left home it took me a day to get out of Florida. That was the one thing that I didn't like. It's like getting locked in.

A MOTORCYCLING HEYDAY

Around 2003-2004, that was the heyday of motorcycling. All of a sudden we had shows like Biker Build Off and Orange County Chopper on TV.

Everybody and their brother had a motorcycle. Some of the people who'd been riding for a long time started bitching about the new riders and all the yuppies with Harleys, but it was a huge boon to the industry. The new riders brought a lot of money into the industry. That money was used by builders and small shops to develop parts that never would have been manufactured otherwise. Someone like me could go to the store and buy parts off the shelf that would have been a one-off fabrication just a few years earlier.

It was insanity. The rallies all hit peak numbers and everyone opened up a motorcycle shop. That just blew me away. And I was right in the middle of it because I'm doing all the rallies and have a lot of friends in the industry. One of my friends was Billy Lane with Choppers Inc. I knew him in Miami, he and his brother. They were really, really cool cats.

THE BILLY LANE CONNECTION

I remember one of my friends would have a party and here come these guys, and they're young, they're really young. They were in their early 20s and they had super hot, smokin' hot South Beach model type chicks with them and it just blew our minds. They had the coolest motorcycles. They were riding Knuckleheads and Panheads and that was way before that was cool. Back in those days the only people that had a bike like that was somebody that knew how to work on it. I don't care how much money you had, you couldn't ride that stuff unless you knew how to work on it.

So they were accepted into the group, into a crowd where really there were no newcomers. You had to spend years proving yourself. Billy and I became good friends and will be forever. You know he was a cool guy. It's an honor to be around somebody like that and I was able to be around him through all that. I remember when he moved to Melbourne and first opened his shop, a bunch of us went to his shop warming party.

If you look at custom motorcycles, what people were doing in the late 1990s, they were building some really cool stuff, but they weren't thinking outside of the box. Not until the early 2000s. That's when builders really started doing some off-the-wall thinking. Billy was one of them that just really did some new things. His stuff was really out there.

I remember going to his first shop party, that's when I realized just how far out there Billy was. I asked him, "What are ya going to do next?" And he showed me some of the projects. One was the first magazine bike that he was doing. He had this square block of aluminum and he'd drawn on it with a marker. He had it duck-taped to the side of a Softail frame and he's explaining, "This is what I'm going to do. I'm going to build it like this and it's going to be a hub-less wheel." I'd never seen that done before. So more and more I'm thinking, this guy is pretty cool and I'm going to stick around and see where he goes.

When Billy's shop started booming with all the TV exposure, he needed more help. I suggested that I haul for him, and I ended up buying a dually truck and pulling his trailer for a season. We went around the country and I did the driving for Billy. It was good. It allowed me to go to these events and be around the action, it subsidized my income while I lived like a rock star the entire time I was gone to all the events.

The other thing it did was introduce me to everybody in the industry. I'd seen some of these people around, but now we're spending time together. On the weekends and during the bike shows, everyone's busy selling their thing, making their appearances. Like politicians, they're shaking hands and kissing babies. I mean that's what you do during a bike rally.

But between rallies, in the heyday, people weren't even going back home. There's no sense in it, you don't have time. The boss might fly in and out, but the crews, they're on the road full time. So during this time, between the rallies, I'm spending time with all the other crews and a lot of industry people and we're hanging out. We're eating together and we're really getting to know each other. During that two-year period I got to know everyone in the industry, that was a turning point in my life.

One of the things that happened during this period, a lot of favors were exchanged. People would have a bike and they'd ask me, "Can you throw the bike in your trailer and haul it to the next show for me?" I'd do favors for people like Kendall Johnson and Indian Larry, and then they owed me favors. It wasn't like we collected on each other, but it was an unwritten thing. So if you got into trouble, I knew that if my bike broke down, they were a phone call away. And that was great. Billy had a lot of people working for him, it was busy and booming and growing even bigger. But like most jobs, even the best jobs, it got old. So Billy ended up going his way and I took a look at some other opportunities.

During my time at the rallies, I came back into contact with an old friend, John Green with Easyriders. When I got clean and sober in 1988 and bought my first Harley David-son, that's when I met John Green. John is a really good guy. Unbelievable guy. At that time he was driving a truck for Easyriders and working for Joe Teresi with Easyriders mag-azine.

Later, Joe split everything up and, unbeknownst to me, John ended up buying the complete event section and the tractor-trailers. John ran everything. He ran the Easyrider Events. When we came back into contact, he ended up offer-ing me a position.

John has these trucks and he explained what he wanted me to do. "Look, here's the deal, I'll bring you on and you can drive." So I started working for Easyrider Events driving a tractor-trailer. They were really cool. They let me haul my motorcycle around with me. My first Job for John was to drive a Peterbilt tractor-trailer from Daytona Beach to Sturgis.

I started driving to all the Easyrider events. I'd done a few of them before I went to work for John, and I thought each one was pretty much the same. But once I got on that circuit, I realized that each location brings it's own spice to the event. The locals give each event it's own personality, especially with the rodeos.

I also helped out with the bike shows. At that time I believe we were doing 26 shows a season. It started on January 4th and went until a week before Daytona, the first or second week in March. That means for all of January, and February there's nothing but show after show after show and it was really pretty stressful.

We stayed out there and we stayed busy, but it was tough. Eventually it got a little old on me. It wore me down. Even John made the comment, "You're not yourself, you're not smiling." It was a tough thing and I ended up leaving, but on good terms. That's when I started to realize, I'd had all these dream jobs that most people would just die over, and I always ended up leaving, so I guess I'm just unemployable.

And in a way that's who I am. I like to have fun. I like to do what I want to do, but I've learned to live in such a way that I don't have to work so much. That was another turning point for me, when I started realizing that I've got to make so much money just to keep up with my overhead. I had a truck payment, a payment on the house in Miami. A cable TV bill and a furniture payment. I bought all this nice stuff to have a nice place and I was never there. For the two years I worked for Choppers Inc. and Easyriders I was living on the road, I would be on the road for two months at a time. When my route took me close to Miami or Daytona I would go home for a day.

Whenever I did get home, the phone calls would start the next day, "Where are you at? Okay, we're going to need you. We're getting ready to do this and that." And I'd be like, "You know what, I haven't been home in two months. I spent one night in my bed, I am going to spend two nights here in a row before I leave." And then I'd be late getting back, just so I could spend two nights in my own bed, only to leave again and be gone for another two months. I did that for two years.

You learn to live a whole different way. You know you gotta keep track of your bills in your head. You have to carry around all these mailing addresses. This was before the Internet, it really hadn't hit yet. At least for me it hadn't. I realize that now you can do everything, like paying bills, on your phone through the Internet.

FIVE

TOO MUCH OVERHEAD

So like I said, the easiest way to deal with my situation was to not have so many bills. I believe it was in 2006 when I sold my house in Miami. I thought I took a big hit and that the housing bubble had burst at that point. But really, the market continued to crash after I sold the house. I could have sold the house for 50% more than I did if I sold it a year earlier. If I had sold it a year later though, I would have sold it for 50% less than what I actually sold it for.

I did make some money on the house, and I took that money and went to Tennessee, because the cost of living is so low there. One of the reasons I bought there was John Green. I asked John, "If you could move anywhere in the U.S., where would you move?" And he said, "I was already thinking about Tennessee. It's centrally located to all these events. It would make life so much easier. And the cost of living is pretty low."

Well I found a place in Tennessee. I had a goal in my life; to build a cabin and maybe have a couple of smaller cabins on the property. That way I would have a spot for my friends to stay and maybe I could rent the extra cabins out to bikers and create some income.

A friend of mine had a place in Tennessee. He'd owned it for a long time and said he didn't live there anymore. I only wanted to buy land, but he was willing to sell me this property for the same amount as the value of the land alone. Now the house was pretty much shot and I had to rebuild the whole thing. It should have been bulldozed, but I'm hard-headed that way and I ended up tearing the entire roof off, then I jacked the house up and leveled it, and then I built a second story. Next, I ripped out the floor downstairs and replaced all that. So pretty much everything got replaced in one way or another, just not all at once.

I did it the hard way. That's what I do; I do everything the hard way. That was in 2006 and I worked hard on it for about six months. When winter rolled in I drew work to a close because I was running out of money. I had good credit though and for a while I thought, I'll just get a loan. Because of the housing market though, the loan people were really being pricks about giving out loans and it couldn't be done. Well, I knew some people with money, so I started talking to individuals about getting a personal loan like I first did when I bought my Miami house.

I figured $60,000 would finish my project, not a lot of money when you're talking about a six bedroom, 6½-bathroom house. I figured the house alone would be worth $200,000 when it was done. Now it's on my property, I own that outright, and it's worth $75,000. So I wanted a loan for $60,000. Theoretically for this loan, the land is worth it, even with the housing bubble, the market value on my property is over $60,000, but it already has a house half built and I was going to finish the house to bring up the value even more with the loan, and I even said I don't need to have it all at once. I can get it in payments as I'm building the house, to secure this loan, to make sure that there is enough equity in the property, so there's no money at risk.

Then I got to thinking, I run the risk of losing the whole thing. The only way I can continue building on the new house and business is to borrow money, which puts me back in the rat race. I built as much house on the new land as I could – and quit when the money ran out.

So then I decided I don't want a loan. Once I made that decision the rest was pretty easy. I don't have a place to live, but until I get the money, I'm just going to take vacation and get around. That was in 2006. I just started doing whatever I want and going where I want and work when I need to eat.

Rather than try to work and earn money to make a dream happen, I'm working a little bit to make just enough money to travel around and survive. My attitude is, it's time to take a vacation until the economy improves. When it improves and I can make money again, then I'll come off vacation. Until then I'm not going to work hard and try to make a square wheel turn. It just ain't happening. So all these different events put me in the position I'm in today and been in for the past five to six years Relax, travel around, do what I can do. When I need money, I work and make a little money. If an opportunity arises and I can make some money, I take the job.

I rebuilt the Tennessee house with no plans. That experience, combined with other construction work I've done over the years, means there really isn't anything I can't do. I do all my own electrical and plumbing, tile work, and roofing, That's what I do now. Before I go someplace I ask myself, where do I want to go? what are my options? What kind of rallies are going on? Now I've got options. Maybe there are 10 possible places to go. Then I put my feelers out to people I know. Do they have any kind of work going on? Do they need help with a construction project? And the next thing you know, somebody calls me up and they say, "Hey, I got this idea for my house, when can you be here?"

And they're usually willing to work with my schedule. Pretty soon I have jobs lined up for the spring, summer, and the fall. Now I know where I need to be, one's in California, one's in Kentucky and let's see, the fall, what am I doing in the fall? Oh yeah, back in California. That's how I plan my way. I know where the rallies are and I also know where the work is and I just try to make it all come together.

THE FUTURE

It might surprise people, but I do try to plan ahead. I always think about some sort of retirement and I joke about it - I still don't know what I'm going to do. That can depress me sometimes, because I don't want to be a burden on people when I grow old. And yet, that's the only thing that I see, unless I have a quick death, which in a way wouldn't be the end of the world.

So there's going to be this transition where I get old and then maybe want to retire. Right now though, other than the bed and breakfast idea, I don't have a good retirement plan. Like everything else it boils down to timing and I'm going to leave it to fate. So yeah, I'm not really planning on a large retirement plan. They joke about Social Security not being there; well I got 15 more years or so, before I'm even vaguely eligible. So I guess if I can stay on vacation for 15 more years, maybe I'll get some income, where I can finally take vacation from taking vacation and rest for my final years.

SIX

BEAN'RE CYCLE

Creating the bike I ride now, the customized Road King, that really began when I first started hanging out with Billy Lane. He invited me on some of his rides including one of the Discovery Channel rides. Everybody had these really cool bikes. They were all outdoing each other with great bikes and here I am riding this bone-stock Bagger. A Road King; the best bike I ever had and the perfect bike for me. It was great, but it had the class of a mini van. You know it was so functional and everything, but it just didn't work in that group.

So I thought about building a new chopper. I even talked to Billy about it. I had a Knucklehead at the time, in addition to the Road King, that I was going to rebuild and customize. I really didn't think that it would work for me though. Knowing the kind of riding I do, the mileage I put in, and the places I go at the drop of a hat. With the Road King, there was never an issue, never a problem. So I thought, I gotta stay with a new bike; I can't run an old-school chopper with an old motor. I was thinking about it and I thought about buying a new bike. Of course the bike I would prefer would be a Road King. Finally I thought, this is stupid, I have a Road King, why would I get another one?

So I decided to customize my Road King, and at that time no one customized Road Kings. This was 2001. No one was doing Baggers. Baggers weren't cool yet. All through

motorcycle history, what people did was bought Harleys –
baggers included - and stripped them down. The first thing
they did was get rid of the windshield and the hard saddlebags and those were some of the things I needed to keep.

Billy's second Discovery Channel Biker Build-Off was
against Dave Perewitz. As part of the build off, we were
going to ride from Louisiana to Dallas, Texas. I told him I'd
be there, so I wanted to do something with my bike before
the ride. I decided to put a longer front end on the Road
King and chop it. I called a buddy of mine, Matt Mihm,
who's a certified welder and I told him what I wanted to do.
He said, "You know that's crazy. You've got a really nice new
bike. What you should do is buy a frame and start there."
And I was like, "Why do I want to buy a motorcycle frame
and save this stock bagger frame? Who the hell wants a stock
bagger frame? I don't care, this is my bike."

THE FIRST CHOP

I bought some extended tubes, six inches over stock,
pulled the front fork apart and installed the longer tubes.
Then I rode over to my friend Matt's house just the way it
was, with the front of the bike way up in the air. It looked
like what people did to Hondas and Triumphs back in the
1970s. Oh yea, I put my Sawzall in the saddlebag when I
headed over to his house.

I told him I wanted to cut the neck and bend it out until
the bike was level and then we'd weld it up, and that's exactly what we did. I put a jack under the frame and jacked
the whole bike up off the ground. Then I started cutting
through the neck and as I got close to cutting all the way
through, all of a sudden the weight of the front end pinched
the saw blade. That's when I stopped cutting, before I'd cut it
in two.

Then we started to let the jack down real slow. As soon as that front wheel hit the ground, it started rolling out and the neck started opening up, the piece of metal at the top of the neck that held the bike together, that acted like a hinge. We kept lowering the bike more and more – and the wheel would roll out and the gap in the neck where I cut it would open up farther. Then we would stand back, take a look, and let it down just a little bit more. Finally, I said, "Okay, right there, weld it up."

The final cut in the neck was a triangle that went from about three quarters of an inch at the bottom to nothing at the top. My buddy welded that all back up and reinforced the neck where we did the cut. That's how we chopped the bike the first time. When it was all done, it looked more like a pro street bike than a chopper. It looked more like what people are doing with their baggers now. You know, they just rake them out and maybe lower the bike and it gives them a great ride. It's also very functional. It's aggressive.

I rode that to Dallas and back for the Discovery Channel ride. I liked the bike, but it didn't get the attention I wanted. But of course you have to look at who I'm riding with. I'm riding with all these people like Billy Lane, and it just didn't stand out enough.

CHOP NUMBER TWO

So I thought, my plan worked the first time, I'm going to try it again. When I cut the neck the first time I didn't take anything off the bike, not even the gas tank. I just cut it and we welded it and that was it. This second time, I got a ten-over front end and put it on my bike, so now the front of the bike was way up in the air again. And once again I rode over to my buddy Matt's house, and he's like, "What do you want to do this time?" And I said, "I'm going to cut through both down tubes and we'll cut the top tube underneath the gas

66

tank." Well, when we took the gas tank off I realized my top motor mount is right there and I didn't want to get into trouble by moving the mount. So I cut the top frame tube in front of the motor mount, then I cut the two down tubes in the middle. Basically I cut the bike into two pieces.

The wiring was an issue though. Road Kings have a big fat wiring harness that runs up into the headlight. There's a gazillion wires and I didn't want to cut all those wires and have to splice them all together again to make the harness longer. So I'm pulling and trying to stretch the wiring harness as far as I could. My goal was to get the front of the frame out and up as far as I could without cutting the harness. The best I could do with the stock wiring harness was five inches up and two inches out. So I said, "This is what we're going to do. We're going to make the down tubes five inches longer," and that's what we did. We put five-inch slugs in the middle of the down tunes and then we welded up the backbone so the bike set level. So I had a frame that was five inches up and two out and I liked that. In fact, that's what I still run today. That's a real good chopper look. If I did this again today though I would go slower and take the time to figure out the rake and trail before welding it all together. I was lucky, it handles great. I can surf – I can stand on the seat and ride the bike with no hands - so you know it definitely tracks good.

The other thing I decided to do was drop the seat. That was something I got from Billy. The oil tank on the Road King is under the transmission, there's nothing structural under the seat. The transmission's all the way on the bottom of the bike. So essentially I could drop it all the way to the top of the transmission. I thought I would have to relocate the battery, bagger's run a big battery, but it turned out there was plenty of room under there. I cut the frame and dropped the seat height and Matt welded the frame tubing back together. That dropped the bottom of the seat three inches without even touching the stock suspension. Then, because I had a custom seat made with thinner padding, I was able to lower the actual seat height another two or three inches. Now I'm sitting about six inches lower than on a stock Road King. The effect, with the seat so low and the gas tank five inches higher, gave the bike really nice lines.

Even though the lines from the side were good, when I extended the down tubes five inches, the view from the front was not great. You've got two tubes that come down at an angle, basically making an A. So when you make the middle of that A five inches longer, there's no way of keeping those lines straight. The down tubes ended up having a kink in the middle. Okay, that looked bad. It looked Frankenstein scary.

The main thing I was worried about though was, how would it ride? So the very first thing I did after Matt and I reassembled the bike, was ride to a 20-year reunion at Camp Lejeune, North Carolina.

One of the platoons in my Company went to Beirut. I didn't get to go, but a lot of my friends were there. So I always supported that and they invited me up for their reunion. I thought perfect; I'll ride up to North Carolina and test the welds. So I rode up to North Carolina for the weekend and came back, everything was fine. It rode and handled great. I loved it. I said, okay, these dimensions will work, but I need to make it better looking. I needed to basically replace both of the down tubes from the neck all the way down to the front motor mount, and where the tubes start to bend.

I liked the way the bike handled and the basic look, but I knew what I needed to do was to completely remove both the down tubes and fabricate two new ones.

My plan was to replace both down tubes with twisted rectangular stock. Using two tubes is important because at

68

that time Indian Larry was doing twisted rectangular tubes in some of his frames, but they were a single down tube design. Larry started with a two inch, solid steel piece of rectangular steel, and twisted it. He would heat it up and do all these twists and reverse twists and it really was cool. Larry had a real good signature twist that he used, very intricate. Well, I didn't want to totally copy Indian Larry. I don't like to copy people. I'll give everyone the credit for the original idea, and that's pretty much what I was trying to do. I'm also lazy, and didn't want to spend the time needed to do it his way.

CHOP NUMBER THREE

I knew the guys who worked in this metal shop in Homestead, Florida. They worked on farm and irrigation equipment. At that time there was a lot of farming in Homestead. The farmers use these giant metal contraptions to irrigate those huge thousand-acre fields. Building and maintaining all that equipment required a lot of welding. Sometimes the guys in the shop would help people with projects like airboats and stuff, but pretty much they worked on irrigation equipment. They had a job, no glamour, just a job. So when they got a chance to work on a bike; I mean, they really thought, oh yeah, that'd be cool.

So I told them I gotta make some down tubes. I'd ridden the bike over there so I could show them. And they said, "Yeah, we can do that." I said, "I want some twisted steel for the down tubes," They said, "How about we make the tubes from one inch sold steel bar stock?" And I'm thinking that'd be great and I wouldn't be copying anyone.

I asked them, "Can you twist the rods?" They said, "Sure, we can twist it." So the guy takes this two-foot long piece of square, one-inch solid stock and he puts it in a lathe, this giant lathe. He locks it all down and then he gets ready to twist it. And I told him, because I'd been watching Larry do all his stuff, "Whoa, you got to heat it up first." He just smiled at me and hit the button on this lathe.

That lathe cold twisted that steel with the greatest of ease. He could easily have spun it like a pretzel until it broke. I mean the lathe was that big and powerful. It was amazing. So he did one. I loved it, I said, "That's cool." So he did another, and I said, "Perfect." He goes, "No, no, no, no, they don't quite match let's do another one." Then he does number three. And before welding them in place, where the new tubes hit the existing frame tubes, they turned the ends down until they were round and just small enough to slide about a half inch into the very bottom of the existing down tubes. At the top we did what's called a butt weld. You just butt the two pieces together and weld them. And it just really came out right. I have Indian Larry to thank for the down tube influence and Billy to thank for the drop seat.

The finished bike already rode and handled great, now it looked great too.

I don't want to say I was the first, because no one's ever the first. There's always someone who did something somewhere along the line, but there were only a very small handful of people who were doing anything like this to a Bagger.

After I did the down tubes correctly, my bike started to get a little bit of notoriety. Scout, the PR person for Baker Drive Train, he liked the bike and was one of the first with the premonition that Baggers were going to be the next big thing. And mind you, this is when fat tire choppers were the in thing.

He used my bike and me in an ad campaign. At the time I only had 175,000 miles on my bike. The campaign was all about the Baker six-speed transmission, the whole pitch was promoting the quality and durability of the Baker transmission – and it is a great transmission. During Sturgis one year he had me go through Spearfish Canyon so they could take pictures for the ads. I went through the canyon I don't know how many times, dragging my floorboards, and he's like, "Can you go a little faster?"

Some years after that you started to see a few more people customizing Baggers. They were starting to rake them out a little bit. Each year, a few more people would spend the money and time to build a really nice Bagger. For whatever reason, what I call Chopper-Baggers started catching on. Now today, the most in thing is a Bagger with a raked out front end, tall tire and a set of ape-hangers. But the bikes are still very functional. These are bikes you get on and ride anywhere you want.

A NEW BEAN'RE CYCLE

Now, I'm really happy with my bike, but everyone keeps saying I need a new bike. And you know, it has almost 300,000 miles on it and it's been broken physically in half numerous times. I broke the swingarm three times. I mean it runs the risk of actually falling apart. J.W. joked that when I retire my bike; all that's going to be left is purple dust. I used to be jealous of the people who lived up north because their riding season stops in October and a lot of them bring their bikes inside the house or garage, tear them down, rebuild them, and make them all beautiful again. And then they bring them down to Daytona. They have pretty bikes. Of course they do, they've got six months to work on them. I don't. I've always tried to live in climates where I can ride year round, even when I'm not travelling; I still want to live there so I can keep riding.

I ride year round, I ride every day. My motorcycle is my only means of transportation and I don't have time to rebuild it. My bike needs nothing less than to be torn down to the bare frame, and put back together correctly – at least partly because it never was built right the first time. I was cutting corners, that's how I work. The other thing is, I don't have the time for the bike to be laid up for a complete restoration. How can I take it apart if I need to keep riding? So I just keep it running. I've been putting Band-Aids on every ailment it's had for years now. What I need to do is start from scratch and come up with a plan to have it down for six months. And although I'd love to do that I'd probably go a little stir crazy without my motorcycle.

I want to keep my bike running and spend three to four months building a new bike. Because I don't have money to do that, and because I know everyone in the industry; I have this idea. Actually, for years now, people have been talking about wanting to build me a bike. And you know that would be an awesome honor for someone to surprise me and hand me a bike, but it's not going to happen.

But I do have a whole bunch of people in the industry willing to lend their expertise and time to help me build a bike that's safe and sturdy. I ride a lot of miles a year, so it has to have certain things. I'm getting older too and you know my body's not forgiving like it used to be, so it has to be comfortable. I can't do a rigid frame. I need suspension. I need rubber mounting. I need a windshield.

I'm going get a lot of the people I know in the business involved. I want to use their products and in doing so, they'll be able to use the bike and me in their ads. It's like an R&D project for them, a long-term product test. I'm not going to use any parts that I don't have full belief in. And I'm not going to use cheap parts like some of the stuff that comes from China.

I'm going to get the best products made by the best people in the business and build a bike that's designed for my kind of riding. If I want to ride 4,000 miles to Nova Scotia, Canada and then to Sturgis, South Dakota, I want a bike that will do that. I want the same bike to be tough enough that when my buddies decide in the middle of the night that we should all go racing, I can join in without hesitation. That when we go out on the dirt track and do hot laps until somebody gets hurt or something breaks, my bike is durable enough to keep up.

When that's all over, I expect to get on my bike and head to Baja, Mexico. That's the kind of riding I do and that's the kind of bike I want to build. Comfortable and dependable. Something that looks good and can still take a beating. I believe there are a lot of American-made quality products out there and I want to incorporate as many of those in the project as I can – a lot of them come from people that I know, friends in the industry who have supported me in the past.

Together we can have another seven years, and 300,000 miles of crazy biker tales and adventures. What a better testimonial to their products, still looking cool and running good after all those miles.

I also know a lot of good fabricators and builders, so anyone who provides parts knows they will be assembled and installed by professionals. I've worked with a few of the big builders. They know better than to let me actually do anything, but they let me be there. Sometimes they might even hand me a welder or something, that's what I'm looking forward to doing, not just having a bike built, but being involved in the build itself. It's everyone's dream.

I know everyone would like to work with the builders and do what I plan to do, so I plan to cover this build. Not only am I going to be reporting the day-by-day and week-by-week progress on building and riding this new bike, I'm also going to be doing interviews and short stories about the people who are helping me out. I want to tell people what it's like to be around the builders and fabricators, and try to give everyone a little taste of life in these shops.

The idea for the build gets bigger and bigger and it's not just about building a motorcycle. This is more than just another bike that's going to be in a magazine for a photo shoot. This is going to be so much more. You will see the bike being built, and you will see the same bike at every rally – because I will ride it to every rally. Maybe it's going to have a dent or two in the tank, because I'm not going to fix those, they're part of the story. That was an important story when that happened. I'll tell you when it happened and how it happened and with who. The bike is going to have a life of its own. And I hope to make everybody a part of that life. With the Internet and magazines and all the social medias, people will be able to see it and live it. Even after the new bike is built, I plan to keep the purple chopper. People talked about it going in a museum and maybe one day it will, but I'm going to hold onto it for now. It'll sit in the background and wait.

LAST MINUTE DEVELOPMENTS

As we go to press a lot of my dreams for the new bike have come together. Like I said earlier, I am fortunate to be able to use some of the best products in the world. These products include a Crazy Horse "V- Plus 100" engine backed by a Rivera Primo six-speed transmission. The wheels are going to be custom "Bean're" wheels created by Renegade Wheels, set in a custom frame from Indian Larry Motorcycles. The sheet metal for this new chopper will come from the crew at Klockwerks and Will Ramsey of Faith Forgotten Choppers. The paint job is going to be a group effort by Darren at Liquid Illusions in St. Louis and Little Jay in Dothan, Alabama.

I have some of the best builders in the world helping me, including Matt Hotch, Aaron Greene, Brian Klock and Sugar Bear, just to name a few. I will also be bringing in a whole lot of other builders and manufactures. You can keep up with the build in Cycle Source or at www.cyclesource.com. It is going to be off the hook, you will be seeing the new bike at all the rallies as I will be riding it everywhere. Of course my friends at Spectro Oil will make sure it keeps going down the road just like my last one has – for over 300,000 miles.

I am also working with a vintage Indian racing team called Team Bean. I will be piloting Shealin Brayton's 1920 Power Plus Indian with crew chief Sean Brayton. Sean has many restoration builds of both cars and motorcycles under his belt as well as a completion in the first Cannonball on his 1911 Indian. We will be racing at a variety of events around the country including stops on the salt flats. A few overseas stops are in the planning stages as well.

Also, I recently started writing a monthly article in Cycle Source magazine entitled "Highway Prophecies - Cosmic Chronicles of a Biker Gypsy." And I've been courted by several TV shows, it seems only a matter of time before I get picked up for a one or the other. As time goes on more and more opportunities are coming my way. Like most things in my life - The way happens if I just get out of the way.

FRIENDS

—

BETSY

- Personal Trainer, Moto-journalist, cast member on Discovery Channel's Motorcycle Women, climber of Mount Everest

In much the same way that there was "Something About Mary," there is most definitely SOMETHING about Bean're. Exactly what the something is has yet to be defined, but it is a quality that sets him apart from the rest. Bean're is not like the others. He recognizes this about himself to such an extent, that if he had to fit in, and be like the others, I think it would actually cause him mental duress!

"When are you gonna break me off a piece of that Kit Kat bar?" Bean're asks. "Ain't never gonna happen," I answer. "Oh, it's GONNA happen," he'd reply with all of the confidence of a man who gets his way all too often. "Ain't never gonna happen," I'd repeat. And we'd both laugh.

I honestly think Bean're tries to break off a piece of Kit Kat bars out of habit more than actual interest. He's a single man, and it's simply in his nature. But I've known Bean for such a long time that it would be like incest to let MY chocolate melt in his mouth! He and I have been on the bike scene for so many years it's hard to say exactly when we met. I just knew "who" he was for years before I knew who he really IS.

Bean're has a wardrobe that could only be worn by a pimp daddy or a rock star. In trying to recall the first time I ever saw him, I do believe he was in a purple suit and top hat inside of the Broken Spoke, which didn't seem odd at the time, because Sturgis has always been the land of the odd, expressing their own sense of self in extravagant ways, myself included.

But, as unusual and extreme as Bean seems, he and I have a few things in common that surprised me. He has been clean and sober for several decades. I thought I was the lone clean and sober wolf in the Black Hills, but here is my male counterpart, stone cold sober, but as wild as wild can be to the point where people would try to cut us off, but there's nothing to cut us off from!

So he looks silly, he acts crazy, he's sober, he rides like the wind and we both love to push each other to our limits on the curvy mountain roads.

He's not only world traveled, but he's educated and well read, served in the military, and funny as hell, but there's something about Bean're you might not know. He's a hopeless romantic, wears his heart on his sleeve, and when he's in love? Utterly and completely faithful. And when love fails him? He gets heart broken beyond consolation.

Bean're and I actually knew of each other for years. But we became friends over our broken hearts for loves gone, well, just plain wrong. I saw a side of the "Mayor of Fun" that I didn't know existed, and I grew to respect him in many ways, and to love and appreciate him like a twin brother of another mother. Who would guess that a guy in a purple pimp daddy suit, on a big ole purple chopper, could lose his mind over love?

And who would guess that when Cycle Source sponsored a day on the Pine Ridge Reservation for a small group of bikers to hang out and play baseball with a group of the Indian Kids, that Bean're would be having more fun than the kids as he piled as many as four kids at a time onto his purple machine as a few of us took turns riding them around and around the lumpy baseball field. The kids didn't want to quit, so we just kept going round and round until the sun went down.

And when he rode half way across the country just to join me for a ride up to the Big Bear Choppers, "Ride the Mountain," event, he melted the heart of my then 76 year old rider friend Grace McKean. They were gabbing for hours as if they were old friends and laughing over each other's stories. Bean definitely has the gift of gab, and an oddly easy way with the ladies. Once when we were way back in the Malibu Hills visiting the "Mash" set on motorcycles, a group of handsome people on horseback were passing us on a narrow path going the opposite direction. Bean's easy going, spontaneous nature had him on the back of a vacant horse that was just being led within seconds of laying eyes on the pretty blonde girl in the back of the group, that ended up being the sister of Bridgette Bardou. Don't worry about me Bean're, I can take care of myself! I love the fact that our friendship is such that I am happy when great opportunities fall into his lap, which they do just seem to do every single time we hang out!

I'm not sure if it's the hair or the hat, his cocky attitude or his devious smile, but Bean're always seems to convince people that he's worth letting in the door! I remember when I was having problems with my VIP connection getting backstage at Steven Tyler, Bean're just happened to be walking by. The security guy who was giving me a hard time asked Bean, "Are you with the band?" and Bean said, "Of course I'm with the band." Then he said, "Okay, you're in charge of her," and with that, Bean're was in charge of where I got to go on the backstage lot. Bean're, in charge of me? The self-appointed Mayor of Fun is in charge of me? I cannot think of a better person to be put in charge, because it's a guaranteed adventure with Bean're. Bean're has the heart of a child, the libido of a teenager, and the riding skills of a man that's been doing what he does longer, better, and harder than anyone else I know. One thing you can never take away from Bean is this: Bean're is the real deal. He lives the life of a nomad biker. You might see him dressed like a clown at an event and think that it's a whole lot of show. But there are 320 days a year between those rallies that Bean're is on some lonely road, alone on that broken down purple chopper, still livin' it. When there are no cameras or magazines, and the rest of us have all gone home to our normal lives, there is still a tent and sleeping bag on that purple bike. The guy is never in the same place for long enough to receive a package that I've been trying to mail for years. I'd sent it to the next place that he is going to be, but for the most part, even Bean doesn't know where that is - until he gets there. He is just out there, following his heart, even when he doesn't know where it's going himself! Vaya con Dios Bean're! Keep livin' the dream!

✪ ✪ ✪

BILLY LANE

– Famous Bike Builder and owner of Choppers Inc.

Life and adventure are out there on the road. Some of us chase them. Others are oblivious to them. But for those among us who see the road as more than a mere route between two points on a map, we find the experiences, the places, and the people that share our lives. We quantify these treasures not by the number of miles we've ridden, but rather in the deep and lasting impressions they've left on our souls.

When I reflect on the many memories I have gathered over the years, I feel a rush of color, chrome, vibration and sound. I've been outrun by many a sunset and chased by the police. There have been trouble-free cross country runs, and break-downs an hour from home. Some faces I may never remember, but some people I'll never forget.

When I meet some one and sense that it is not just A passing occurrence, I wonder when and how our paths will cross again. And how often. That kind of thinking becomes part of how I identify with a person in a way which will allow us to become more than simple acquaintances – possibly friends or brothers.

Meeting Bean're, I remember wondering why our lives hadn't intersected earlier. I'd been riding for years by that point, and Bean're already had a significant head start on me.

We found that we shared many mutual friends, and had put our kickstands down in the same gravel more than once – just never at the same time. We began seeing each other, suddenly it seemed, frequently at various bike events around the country.

I realized that Bean're was and is one of the special and rare few people who is in it for life – and for all of the right reasons. He is damn near as recognizable as the bar and shield, and his laugh can overwhelm a set of shotgun pipes. If you've seen Bean're – with the top hat, cigar and mustache – you'll find him instantly familiar. If you know Bean're, you know you will find him on the road.

✪ ✪ ✪

BOB SEEGER JR.
– Manager of Indian Larry Motorcycles

I first met Bean're while he was hanging around Billy Lane and the Choppers Inc. boys and girls at Biketoberfest in Daytona around 2003. I really didn't know what to make of him, he's a big, long-haired guy, tattoo'd, with the Choppers Inc. tank-top, then t-shirt, then jacket all layered with a Choppers Inc. hat. A true company man. I've always liked the way Bean're carries himself, like a man should but most don't, honest and straight forward.

When attending motorcycle shows all over the United States, working with Elisa my AWESOME wife and business partner and our partner Indian Larry, I'd see Bean're and he was always cruising around like the gypsy he is. We would sit and shoot the shit about what's what and the characters we'd see on the streets, then about events going on around the world and what we'd change, if we could.

Indian Larry Legacy was a version after Larry passed and we were still invited with open arms around the world to events and shows. I was telling Bean're how I had an idea on doing our own road shows and I wanted him to be apart of it.

The package was four bike shops, some motorcycle artwork and fun. All in a package that would travel in the 'States and abroad called Grease Monkey Mayhem. Elisa and I figured most people that couldn't leave their state or maybe their country would be able to see cool motorcycles and artwork they'd only seen on TV or inside a few magazines. Bringing Bean're in was a no-brainer, he wanted some lime-light and after all, he is a character.

So we did a lot in Sturgis with a few Heavy Hitters in this business, yeah it was something else. 100'x150' and a party that ROCK'D on Thursday night. The goal was to work on sponsors and change the way business was going for a bunch of us, as if we eat off the same plate. The thing is, not everyone thinks this way (we've learned the hard way). Bean're's roll was kind of like being a mayor of some sort, to bring people in that were out in the streets. The lot was successful in most areas, we were picky with our sponsors, but we were able to do Sturgis Grease Monkey Mayhem for four years and then came Europe.

The ball was rolling and everyone wanted in on a European tour, to say the least. Elisa and I laid out the map; land in Germany, start at Custom Chrome Europe (CCI), our best sponsor. We had a container that was loaded in Brooklyn with bikes from our shop, Indian Larry's, then Cole Foster's bikes then some of Jeff Decker's bronzes and some of his collector bikes.

Elisa did everything, from finding sponsors to getting all the paperwork done for shipping and customs (this is a huge job, many can't handle it, Elisa is a professional). We headed-out from CCI in Germany to the Super Rally in Denmark, then back to CCI for a barbecue and party before we ended up in Italy.

Chianti Hills in Tuscany, Italy was the second event we attended. It is a beautiful place to go to. The south of France was our third event, each one was something special. Business was good all around from doing this, and I drove Bean're nuts the whole way. He drove the semi with everything in it the whole time, we would get lost in some small town and I could still hear his bitchin'. I would laugh and keep leaning out the window putting stickers up all over the poles from town to town then city to city.

We shelved going away with a few shops since some don't want to put legwork in, but it's OK, we intend to slide the books off the shelf on Grease Monkey Mayhem and get out to South America, Australia, Dubai, South Africa, Japan and all of Europe starting in 2013 with an awesome show in Verona, Italy. We will of course be attending events in the Beautiful United States of America. The NYC bike show in the Javits convention center in January every year is the all time best, we will bring a version of Grease Monkey Mayhem to the table there. The cast of characters will change every few shows, since change is good.

My Family, then Indian Larry Motorcycles and Genuine Motorworks, all in Brooklyn, NY, are first. Then it's the great open road. Bean're will be in attendance and working the crowd in his ways and pushing his best selling book, after all not many could keep up with a Real Man like Bean're.

Thanks for the laughter & good-times!

Bobby Seeger, Jr
Indian Larry Motorcycles
AIDAN JACK FOREVER!!

CHARLIE "THE NOMAD"
- Writer for The Horse Backstreet Choppers Magazine

Sometime somewhere along the road I met Bean're. Perhaps it was at the Smokeout when we first raced minibikes together, or maybe it was Sturgis. Was it Daytona? Or maybe it was in the Wal-Mart parking lot in Tennessee. It's hard to say. It could have been anywhere, really. At this point, I couldn't isolate the exact time at which we became friends, but I know it happened over the span of several years. I remember seeing him all over the place before I actually met him. He definitely has his own thing going on which kind of makes him pretty hard to miss. In the course of getting down the road, usually you see nothing but new faces and people you have never seen before and will not likely see again, but periodically you encounter someone who stands out from the crowd, (sort of like "Where's Waldo?" but in an ocean of black leather) and upon seeing them in numerous places that are quite spread out over the course of several years it kind of starts to feel like the whole reason for going somewhere is to hang out with these friends that just so happen to be scattered to the four winds. Even if that's just the excuse needed to keep oozing down the road on whatever has two wheels and happens to be running, it's plenty reason enough. When you find yourself running into the same lanky, smiley, long-haired cat in a top-hat riding a long-ass raked-out purple sled with the vast majority of his worldly possessions strapped to the back, you can't help but notice him. It's pretty safe to say that Bean're stands out from the crowd a little more than just a little.

So often, people have these crazy pre-conceived notions that started in Hollywood back in the late 1940s that every guy on a motorcycle is some super hard bad-ass beer-swilling barbarian type bent on the total destruction of all that comprises conventional suburban life. These notions have managed to embed themselves into the minds of the general public, and taken hold to a quite absurd and stereotypical degree. However, this is fairly deviant from the actual reality of the situation, as far as I've seen it.

While many guys who have motorcycles want to posture themselves in the image of the role that Hollywood has typecast for them over the years, like they are the toughest guys on the planet. Wanna-be outlaws dressed up like brand new bank robbers to go across town on their bikes and have coffee and chain-smoke. Bean're is far more likely to be dressed up in a purple zoot suit with his trademark top-hat in the fashion of the caricature he has kind of become over the years, or in a dress, or a super-hero costume, or who knows what. But whatever he's wearing, you can guaran-damn-tee he'll be kicking that purple sled on down the road to the next spot where the fun is hiding. What it comes down to it, he doesn't take himself too seriously, and that is important. Life is way too short to take yourself that seriously, and in the great grand scheme of things, if something isn't fun or leads to fun or have SOMEthing to do with fun, is it really worth doing? Bean're, also known as the "Mayor of Fun," clearly is successful in the pursuit of all that which is fun. If there really is a Big Rock Candy Mountain, I think Bean're would be the one to ask for directions.

Returning back to the bullshit Hollywood notions of general motorcycle bad-assery and the general public's cultivated fear of what a lot of people refer to as "the lifestyle," what they really fear is the idea that maybe there is a better way of being than staying put in the little corner of life so many people paint themselves into. Motorcycles are freedom machines. When you are riding a motorcycle, you are doing JUST that. You aren't doing ANYthing else but riding, as a matter of course, and the singularity of this pursuit tends to turn the volume down on everything else as your attention is focused more on what you happen to be doing at the moment. And THIS is the underlying vibe of why anybody rides a motorcycle, whether they know it overtly or not. The spontaneity, the fear, and the momentum is truly intoxicating, and terminally addictive. The more you do it, the more your entire world seems to revolve around your motorcycle, since you do what you do so that you can get back on your bike and keep getting down the road. It becomes an obsession, and a singular occupation in and of itself.

So you say Bean're doesn't have a job, do you? He has his big purple motorcycle, and those things definitely don't ride themselves, or fix themselves after they get broken. So you can scratch that one right off of your list of complaints.

Full-on tramping around isn't as easy as it looks, and can be a full-time job in and of itself. You have to sacrifice most of the nuances and many of the comforts of conventional life that the nameless masses so deftly take for granted, in order to pursue your vocation of tramping to the degree of which Bean're is committed. You may have no idea where you are going, exactly, or how it'll shake down when it's all over, but you know you'll enjoy the ride and keep on doing the damn thing, and that's kind of all anybody can really strive to do in life in general. Straight tramping may not pay well in the financial context, but it pays off in spades when you consider fun, experiences, memories, and general satisfaction you invariably take away with you when you get down the road on a motorcycle. Now, consider this carefully - both may be viewed as forms of wealth, but one form can be taken away from you one way or another, and the other form is explicitly yours, that you can take with you and keep in your mind until the final fragile day comes to pass when inevitably we all shed this mortal coil?

So now that we've firmly established the occupation of the creature known as Bean're, which is the straight-tramping Mayor of Fun and full-time committed caretaker and mechanic for one particular giant purple chopper, let us return to the most salient quality of his, that which enables his shenanigans to continue indefinitely. That quality which I am referring to is his attitude. No matter where I have seen him over the years, he always has a positive attitude, no matter how shitty or bleak things may seem on the surface, and this is quite possibly his greatest asset. Life is way too short and fun to focus on the gloom and doom, and conventional demands of the "real world" to such a degree to which one may not be able to capture and enjoy the day at hand. And additionally, attitude can change the fundamental shape of reality. Perception is the universal modifier, and we all have the power to manipulate reality, whether we are consciously aware of it or not. The secret of this power is that; the way we choose to perceive and interpret life ultimately creates its own reality. If we choose to see things as bad, boring, and ugly, then our lives will be just that. Negativity ultimately begets more negativity, until the snowball starts a full-on avalanche of soul-crushing ugliness. If we choose to see things as fun, interesting, and exciting, then reality will be manifest exactly as such, and the world continues being a big and beautiful place, filled with wonder and fun. Hence, it's obvious that attitude is everything in the context of cultivating a true sense of liberty. Although it is quite simple, it's often easier said than done when dancing through the quagmire of the conventional demands imposed upon us by the "real world." Bean're is an example of what is possible if you can fully shake the majority of those demands. If you can get gone, roll with the punches and go with the flow, and maintain a positive attitude regardless of your current situation while doing it, then true liberty can be cultivated and achieved.

It is widely known that freedom has its price, and the nature of freedom at large is no different than the nature of wealth that we have discussed previously. Any freedom that can be given or taken away is not true freedom, as the truest sense of freedom can only be personally manifested within the countenance of the individual, even if it is only recognized by the one who possesses it. It doesn't just happen on its own, you have to make it a priority, and this pursuit of freedom and fun is the Bean's main priority. Sure, he'll have to do some work here and there to get a little cash to get down the road, but without kids, a mortgage, or any of the 10,000 things that people usually drop their loot on, how much money does a guy really need? A committed relationship with a motorcycle really isn't that costly in the great grand scheme of things. Just like any relationship, the bike gets what it wants in the end so that it continues to give you what you want. It's a small price to pay, relatively speaking for a relationship that is at the very least as rewarding as any other. So what else does a guy need money for aside from consumables if he's already got a motorcycle and freedom, and the time to enjoy them both together? You can't buy back time, after all. A guy has to hustle his way on down the road, since gas and oil and tires and food usually don't come for free. For instance, when Bean're hit town in Phoenix a couple years back, he ended up staying at my house for a spell and put a whole new roof on it while he was there to make a little cash to get down the road - and did a fine job at that, might I add. It was during this time that I actually got to know Bean're to a greater degree than I had in the context of us just running into each other on the road. He's a great guy, and a pleasure to have around, not to mention he's pretty handy when it comes to carpentry at large. He's helpful, considerate, and funny. My ol lady Jill loves him, He's like her older brother. For that matter, all the ladies seem to love Bean're. Hey, a guy can't help it if he's got it going on!

The Bean's existence is proof positive that the road goes on forever, and it's bounty remains for all that pursue it. The pursuit of which by means of the two-wheeled persuasion is by far preferable to any of the alternatives available for your average guy to do so. It's clearly possible, and within your grasp. So, what are you waiting for? Get up and take your happy ass for a ride! Time waits for no man in its foul march directly into oblivion. Go drink in the sunshine and speed while it's still outside waiting for you! You can read the rest of this book next time you stop! HAHAHAH!

-el nomad

✪ ✪ ✪

CHRISTINE SOMMERS

-Simon Christine Sommers-Simon - Three-time Motorcycle Hall of Fame inductee, Doobie Brothers wife, Co-Founder of Harley Women magazine, author of The American Motorcycle Girls Cannonball Dairy.

Being around the motorcycle scene for many years I thought I knew most of the more colorful characters who enjoy our lifestyle. Then I started noticing photos in various publications of a brightly dressed, handsome looking dude wearing a large hat. I saw him at a few rallies and his contagious smile. Hmmm... I thought to myself, 'Who IS this guy?'

I didn't see him again for a while, but my friend Mike Lichter introduced us a few years ago in Sturgis. He was super nice and it seemed like he was everywhere. If Patch Adams rode a motorcycle, he would look a lot like Bean're.

I was a rider on the 2010 Motorcycle Cannonball Cross-Country Ride on my 1915 Harley-Davidson. This was the ride of a lifetime! We pulled into Chattanooga, TN, tired and exhausted and there he was, on his purple chopper - of course, purple! What other color would it be? He became one of us, helping out where he could and cheering us on all the way. We shared some crazy moments on the adventure and bonded over bad meals and road grime. I later realized his whole LIFE is one adventure. Talk about living the dream! Bean're IS a walking, talking, motorcycle riding professional tourist and a true inspiration to all of us to 'Live your Dreams.' In this short time we have on this earth, it's a pretty good message.

✪ ✪ ✪

CODY MARKS
- musician with a self-titled band

Bean're is envied from cubicles to service centers all over the world.

People want to live his life, most do not have the balz.

He epitomizes America in the way that he is free.

He's not cheap, he is free

When he is talking to you, you are the only person on the planet at that moment.

He cares about all people and if you are called a friend, be honored.

DAVID UHL

– Famous painter of motorcycles and motorcycle situations.

I have been to enough events over the last 20 years to have seen the man in the top hat many times. I had not been formally introduced until Michael Lichter did the honors at the Broken Spoke one night as Bean're was bartending.

I thought, cool, finally get to meet someone who has left a visual imprint so many times before. Well, a few years passed and then I ran into him again and he looked at me and said, "Stingray wallet." I said, "Huh?" He said again, "You have a stingray wallet." I said, "Wow, your memory is amazing!"

And that was the beginning of what has become a great friendship and an epic oil painting! I am required to be at a number of rallies and events by the nature of my work, and I have to declare that most everywhere I go, I am delighted to see my friend with the massive memory. At one point I speculated there must be at least three or four Bean'res to be at so many events around the globe simultaneously. But now I think he just rides the paint off that purple pan! Godspeed Mr. Bean're!

❂ ❂ ❂

GILBY CLARKE

- Guitarist and record producer best known for his three-year tenure as the rhythm guitarist for Guns N' Roses.

I can't remember the first time I met Bean're. He's the kinda guy you do remember meeting, but I've been on so many bike runs, parties, and all the rest, that it's hard for me to remember at which event I met someone. I know I've seen him at Sturgis and the El Diablo runs, but introductions in our biker contingent are usually "hey." I do remember seeing that purple monster riding along on the last EDR, talking to him over the bonfire on the beach of the Sea of Cortez and he seemed a pretty likable chap. For such a big fella, he's pretty mellow and easy to talk to. I like that in biker circles you can just say "hey, cool bike" or "you really ride a purple bike?" and you have a new friend without misconceptions.

Rock 'n roll Bean're!

✪ ✪ ✪

GLENN MORGAN

- Producer of V-Twin TV and many other films and television shows. Currently working on Project Runway and The Real World. Glenn also co-owns ProItalia, a Ducati dealership in Los Angeles

"Let me tell you about my favorite dream. You've probably had it too. It's the one where you don't have a job, and you just ride your bike to all the best rallies across the country, and you meet and hang out with all the coolest people along the way. You know, that dream. We're not exactly sure how he does it, but we found a guy who lives that very dream."

That was the introduction I wrote to a video piece I produced a few years ago for V-Twin TV. I was working for Easyriders magazine, and we had a deal to air the show on Speed Channel. I was looking for great bikes and people and places to put on the show. So I had the idea to do a segment on a gypsy biker, the kind of throwback guy that was maybe just be a memory from the 70's. But first I had to find someone who fit the bill. I asked my colleagues at Easyriders, as well as people I met at Sturgis. And I kept getting one simple answer: Bean're.

Bean're? I tracked him down and met him briefly at Sturgis. He seemed like a good guy, despite his slightly silly looking bike with the bass boat paint job, so I signed him up to be on the show. We next met at the rally in Chillicothe, Ohio, with camera crew in tow. First, I interviewed some other people who knew him, including builders Paul Cox and Kendall Johnson, and I was amazed at how much everyone loved him. It's like they'd always been itching to talk about him – not just his cool lifestyle, but what a swell guy he is. It seemed like everyone who knows him had a story about the time Bean're rode 200 miles in the rain (at night) when they needed help on the side of the road, or something equally selfless and heroic. And they were all jealous of him, but in a totally positive way: filled with awe instead of resentment at how he lives his life.

I headed out with Bean're and the film crew into "the zoo" campground, and I knew I had found the right guy. He was wearing his "anti-biker" outfit (just to confuse and confound people), a purple pinstripe suit with matching tie and bowler hat. And no one could resist talking to him. If I wore that outfit, I'd get beat up and tossed out on my ass in about five minutes, but Bean're disarms everyone with his humor and unqualified friendliness. He simply loves everybody for exactly who they are. He's the biker Mr. Rogers. He's just as eager to make friends if you're a grizzled one-percenter, a stranger on the side of the road, a prudish grandma who's afraid of tattoos, or an over-educated Hollywood producer-type like me.

The TV piece we did turned out great, primarily because we did a good job of capturing Bean're's essence. How can anyone not like him? And not want to be like him – if only a little bit, for a little while? We've kept in touch over the years, and my admiration has only increased. Oh, and he can flat ride that silly looking bike. He wasn't "putting on" for television, though I've met my share who were. He's the genuine article, not just as a biker, but (dare I say it) as a person. And he seems to be one of the most beloved people I've ever known. Deservedly so.

As I wrote about him originally, "More than anything, Bean're is just the kind of guy you'd like to hang out with." Absolutely. And as Kendall Johnson put it, "Bean're is one of the few guys I know who's got it all figured out."

We need more people like Bean'er. He makes the world a happier place.

GREG SCHEUER

– Edge – Promotions manager for The Horse Backstreet Choppers Magazine and Smoke Out Motorcycle Rally

I've known Bean're for over a decade. I've ridden the Long Road from Arizona to North Carolina with him and a bunch of shorter rides. We've had many good meals. I want to tell you how to take care of Bean're.

Sometimes people meet him and think, "What's that really attractive young lady doing with that old guy?"

Well first, Bean're is younger than he looks - hard living. Secondly, every super-hero has some form of Achilles heel, kryptonite. These young women are his kryptonite. I have known him long enough to see these women arrive and depart, each time leaving Bean're almost financially broke and a bit damaged. So as friends of Bean're, I think we need to keep attractive women away from him. It might be more difficult than you think, but we owe it to Bean're.

❂ ❂ ❂

JACK MCINTYRE

- Owner of Bikerpics, the one-stop shop for bike, event and chick pics.

It was probably back in or around the year of 2003 that I first ran into Bean're in Daytona during the Willies Tropical Tattoo Bike show. He was dressed to kill, and of all that were there his presence was noted. Being a fairly new photographer at the time, I grabbed a shot here and there as we seemed to meet up at the events in the area. Year by year, East Coast or West, where ever the action was, so was Bean're. Charity events, organized rides, I always knew that I was going to have an additional gallery for my site simply based on the colorful images that Bean're provided for us all. I do have a few favorites of course. Grabbing the shot of

Bean're and Steven Tyler at the Michael Lichter exhibit in Sturgis trading hats, smokin' his pipe during the burnout contest at the Buffalo Chip oh so calm and collected, and then having the opportunity to stick with him for a full week as we rode from NYC to Nova Scotia for the Wharf Rat Rally in 2012. What an experience, great group of riders, an area of Canada new to me, very cool. To me, the biker lifestyle is like no other. It's freedom, entertainment, good to your fellow man, and more. Bean're exemplifies all that I just mentioned and more. He shares his never ending tour of this world with the images to match captivating us daily on social media sites such as Facebook. I for one look forward to his travels and the reports from... and once in a while, the opportunity hits and we get to ride together with cameras capturing all. Long live Bean're, our lifestyle needs him.

✪ ✪ ✪

JAY ALLEN

- Possibly the World's Best Motorcycle-Event MC, former owner of the Broken Spoke Saloon, current owner of Jay Allen's Roadshow, and serious motorcycle nut.

My name is Jay Allen and the one thing I haven't been short of in my life is CHARACTERS! One of those characters is a cat named Bean're. In many respects, he's living the dream, but like most things in life, its harder than it looks. Lucky for Bean're he has lots of talents to keep this tumble weed rolling through life on his two wheeled stead from one adventure to another. When our paths cross it's always a good time.

Speaking of talents, this free spirit is one hell of a carpenter, there's not much he can't build. Need your 18 wheeler driven cross-country with $100,000 worth of custom motorcycles inside? Bean're is your man. I'll never forget the day Discovery bike builder Billy Lane asked Bean're if he would drive his rig from Sturgis to Melbourne Fl. With all his bikes. I barely knew him at the time and I WAS FLOORED, looking at this Scooter Bum giving Billy the thumbs up. I knew then that he was not only trust worthy but could get the job done. Since then, Bean're has helped me many times with my mission of developing the Worlds Largest Biker Bar, the Broken Spoke Saloon.

When our work day was over, it was time to ride and boy can Bean're jockey a motorcycle! With 17 Land Speed Records under my belt, I'm not a bad rider myself and it's always a treat to roll with someone who has the ability to ride tight but SAFE. I've ridden some of the curviest roads in the US, from the Redwoods in Northern California to the sweeping turns that crisscross the Black hills of South Dakota, at high rates of speed with this colorful character and hope that our journeys collide many more times in this short life. I'm losing a lot of Brothers as I get older and with our MAYOR OF FUN living so close on the edge of life, my wish is that he may forever KEEP THE SHINY SIDE UP AND THE RUBBER SIDE DOWN. Love Ya Bean're!

✪ ✪ ✪

KEVIN "TEACH" BAAS
- The man who made Chopper Building an accredited high-school class.

Bean're is one of those guys you always look forward to seeing when you're out on your Motor-sikle. He's guaranteed to bring a smile to your face and create a good time when he is around. I love riding my old knucklehead across country, and it seems no matter where I go or what event I'm at, there he is riding in on his purple stallion with a smile on his face wearing some crazy outfit. I have huge love and respect for Bean're and the lifestyle he lives. The man is the real deal and has a heart of gold.

MICHAEL LICHTER

- World's best and best-known photographer of bikes,
bike events and all the people who make up the
motorcycle culture.

Bean're and I officially met on the Billy Lane - Dave Perewitz Jacksonville to Dallas Biker Build-Off in 2003, even though I'd seen him around the scene earlier. From this point on we were off to the races, seeing each other all around the USA (and overseas as well) at the largest and smallest of events, as well as places out of the public eye. Through my lens I've had the pleasure of photographing this larger-than-life character from a distance and up close, have shared enough experiences to say we are truly friends and (believe) I can say I am starting to understand him. I'll take all of him, whether it is the outrageous performing Bean're in his purple pimp suit, paisley smoking jacket, gladiator armor and superhero costumes or the more private, out-of-the-public-eye Bean're at dinner or shredding a steep, bumpy slope on a snowboard. He will be the first to sign up for something, regardless of possible consequences and how outrageous it may be, if it sounds like a fun time no matter. In any form, he has to be the most fun-loving, uninhibited person I know and his contagious smile and laughter brighten so many people's day. Despite walking (and two-wheeling) this earth for more than four-decades, working incredibly hard and helping people along the way, this biker Gypsy has managed to keep that child-like appreciation of the world around him that I have to say I envy. It seems while many people become jaded with their years, Bean're just becomes more of Bean're, and for that I applaud him. My wishes are with him, that he keeps this wonderful attitude forever and infects everyone he touches with some of it. I do believe this world would be a better place if we all followed the lead of Bean're, the "Mayor of Fun."

WOODY
- Owner of the infamous Buffalo Chip

I suspect in everyone's life there is one or two times we just have to ask ourselves, "What the heck is that?" Or just, "Who was that masked man?" Or, in this case, it was a less earth-shattering, "Who is that guy wearing the top hat and that funny suit?"

It seemed, after a few years, that this guy with the funny taste in clothes was at every party at almost every motorcycle event I went to. It didn't seem to matter which coast I was on, or on no coast, like Cincinnati, or Daytona or Sturgis. He was always smiling, and was always surrounded by a crowd of folks who appeared to be having a good time.

I was pretty sure he attended a lot more parties than just the ones I saw him at, too. How else would a top hat show up in those photos in the biker mags? I'm not particularly extroverted and don't make acquaintances nearly as often or as easily as I intend to in my next life. But my curiosity led me to suspect I might meet this unique gentleman in my present life, to look forward to it, and wouldn't you know it happened just like that.

I bumped into Bean're. Or perhaps a mutual friend introduced us. Already I don't recall, though it was probably both, since we seemed not infrequently to find ourselves at the same event. It turns out there's nothing funny about his top hat or other taste in clothing at all. "The Mayor of Fun" he says he is, and I see no one disputing the title.

Smiles are contagious, particularly when spread by such a worldly and unpretentious fellow who's always willing to extend himself to others. We're all pretty pleased that this "Worldoridr" now hangs and parties with us at the Chip. We like to think he's now become the Buffalo Chip's own Mayor of Fun. We know he is one who truly does.

Ride Free & Takes Risks

harf Rat Rally, Digby Nova Scotia

103

105

107

Town of
CAREFREE

elevation 2,5

EIGHT

HOW DO I DO WHAT I DO?

There is one question that everyone asks: how do I do what I do? That question is usually framed around another series of questions: Did I win the lottery? Am I a trust fund baby? How can the average person do it?

Most people believe it's impossible and truthfully it is. For me, I just have to do this. I have to put myself out there. The hardest part of jumping off a cliff is that first step, after that it's pretty easy, you don't have to worry about it anymore. You're going down hill and that's kind of what this is.

MONEY

Money is a funny thing. I believe it is a true curse. I know we all need money to live to a level. If we have a family, we need it even more as we want the best for them. I don't have a family so that makes it a lot simpler for me, but it can still be very confusing.

I have to have gas money and I have upkeep on the bike - like tires. Sometimes I put used ones on. This is not recommended and can be dangerous, but they are free. Sometimes I get takeoffs - a newer tire that was taken off by a shop to put on a different tire. These are near-new and feel good. Still other times I run brand new ones whether they're a sponsored item or I just happened to have the money at the time. Now, I love a new tire and if I could get a new tire every time, I just might start wanting the Best tire there is. That means I need twice the money though. Mounting that new tire is a hassle too, so I'll just keep paying someone to change it. Pretty soon I need a job to pay for all this and I'm working more than I am riding just to pay for my lifestyle that I'm not even living anymore.

This example may seem a bit extreme, but that is how my mind works. Money is a curse for me, though I know it's a necessity. One of the reasons for this book is to generate money so that I can keep riding and therefore keep following my path.

To keep the whole money thing in check, one of the things that I like to do is camp. I call it, keeping it real. I will pull off on the side of the highway, ride down a trail where no one could accidentally come across me or the bike, and spend the night in my sleeping bag. It is a free thing, costs nothing and I don't need to depend on anyone for a place to stay. It makes me appreciate it when I do get a room at a motel or stay on a friend's couch.

And this brings me back to the basics, a place to live. Once you get rid of the place to live, the rest is easy. The house that I'm building is unfinished and 100% unlivable. It does not even have windows yet. It does not have doors.

So, there's not a lot waiting for me there and that keeps me out on the road. It is a major commitment, because I can't fall back on anything. So if something's not going well where I'm at, well I gotta make something happen. I can't just go home. The other thing is, I don't have a safety net of credit cards anymore, due to the economy again. I have bad credit. I've always struggled to keep good credit and it's unfortunate that my credit rating isn't very good. So I don't have good credit. Again, that makes it easier on me. I've given up trying to keep up with the credit card payments. I lost my safety net, but I make what little bit I can to get by and keep going. I really rely on friends a lot. With the help of the Internet, I have a lot more friends, already I probably have at least 1,000 friends that I know all over the United States. So everywhere I go there are people who help me out, and I could not do it without their help.

PROFESSIONAL HOUSEGUEST

I've been told that I'm a professional houseguest. A lot of people have told me that. When I go to your house and stay for a few days, I'm real careful to watch for the warning signs that I'm getting on your nerves or maybe you're getting on mine. It's happened where I didn't see it coming and all of a sudden I'm a major inconvenience and I gotta move on right now. Which I don't mind, but I hate to move on and burn a bridge or leave any kind of animosity or bad feelings behind. Unfortunately that's what happens when you stay at someone's house one day too long.

I stay with people and when it's time to go, it's time to go. Lately when I leave people, I'm sad, I don't want to leave. I don't know what that is now, but I miss them as soon as I leave. It's the way I have to live, it's something that's in my blood. I get fed up with trying to make a more conventional life work. I always choose the inconveniences of traveling and sometimes having to camp in the rain or ride my motorcycle in the cold. Rather than stay in one place, I keep moving.

Sometimes, I'll say, okay, I'm going to take a break now for the summer, or maybe for the winter. Just hang in one place. And within a day or two I figure it out real quick, it's like wow, I'm not moving.

I was just talking to Panhead Billy the other day – Billy's another professional vagabond - and he said he was going to take the summer off and stay west coast. Usually he goes to California for the winter and then he rides around the country in the summer, but he said he's going to take it off and stay in California. You know, I listen to him and I hear myself in that story and I know it's not going to be two or three weeks and that road-jones is going to call and Billy will have to answer it - and I gotta answer it. People like Billy and me, we're not meant to be in one place right now.

Now that being said, I'm sure if I met the right girl, settling down would look different. I've never met the right one or I'd be settled down. I've been happy for a period of time, and I believe it's possible. I've just not met the right one yet. I'm just going to keep doing what I'm doing and keep traveling around.

John Green with Easyrider Events, he said one time that it's in our blood, you know it's that rambling blues thing and I think it's not just being a biker gypsy, there's a lot of occupations that require almost constant travel. Flight attendants, that's a real good one. I mean they know. They got to go. To quit a job like that and just get a regular 9 to 5 would be astronomically hard for most of them. People always say I can't have a relationship doing what I'm doing. Well, flight attendants have relationships.

Musicians are another example. A musician that goes on tour, you know that's tough on a relationship, but it doesn't mean it can't be done. There's plenty of travelling people who have perfectly good functional relationships. Maybe the real question is, why do I do what I do?

PHILOSOPHY

I'm getting to the point where now it might not be so much of what I'm looking for, but the quest. The end product isn't the answer to my question. The travels are the answer.

The quest is the answer. Just out there searching – it's not what I'm going to find, it's the fact that I keep searching and finding out more and more stuff. That is where I'm getting my happiness, to be able to meet the people that I'm meeting, while I'm looking. Be able to let life guide me, rather than saying okay, I'm going to go here now. I say okay, I'm going to get on my bike and go in a certain direction, but I might not end up that way. I might end up riding 180 degrees in the opposite direction. But that is the beauty of it, life calls me that way.

Life guides me. It didn't push me and I didn't pull it, it just kinda steered me this way and that's not just a geographical direction, but a spiritual direction. When I meet the people that I meet, it's not necessarily by accident. I believe everyone meets for a reason and I wouldn't be meeting these people and spending time with them if there's weren't a reason. Maybe it's for me to help these people or do something for them. Maybe it's not. There are certain people that we meet and you know we'll never see again - we aren't meant to see them again and that's okay. But we were meant to meet.

These are just all these people I come across. It's truly a gift to be able to do what I'm doing, and I believe there is so much more going on than I can ever put all in a book. It would take ten volumes of books to really explain.

I meet someone and maybe I only pick up on one small character trait of theirs, but that is their shining quality and that's the one thing that I really liked about that person.

It becomes the one little thing that I want to incorporate into me and now that I've met hundreds of people, I've taken a little piece from every one of them. It's taken all those little pieces from all the people I've met to make a whole Bean're. To make me a whole person. That's what I've got out of this life I'm living.

I think other people can learn from me as well. I don't want to be hypocritical and tell people how to live, but if they watch me and pay attention to what I'm doing, maybe there's one thing that they can do too. You know it's a scary proposition.

I met this young couple when I was in Australia. They were just married and starting their new life together. He had a job, they'd bought a house, they were doing the American dream in Australia. They paid a lot of attention to me. At the time it was MySpace and they watched me on the Internet and they were following my travels. They said I inspired them.

Years later I got an email from them; they were thinking of selling their house, chucking everything and heading out on the motorcycle. And I was like, oh whoa, easy. Are you sure you want to do that? This is a big step and blah, blah, blah. Years later, I got another email from them, they sold everything, chucked it, were riding around on their motorcycle somewhere in South America. And they said they were in one place and couldn't leave right away because they were trying to make a little money. They'd had a few little bike problems, but they were loving it, the life.

I don't want someone who's inspired by me to do something rash and then find out that they really messed up and they can't go back to their old life and they can't get their old job back. But this particular couple, they were living the life under less-than-ideal circumstances. Yet they were very happy and they just wanted to thank me. I'll hear from them again, maybe I won't, but you know, it makes me feel good.

I always feel good inspiring anybody even if I just inspire them to ride a motorcycle. Maybe the fact that I stopped smoking inspired them not to smoke. I think that's huge and I take that as a big honor. That's more than enough inspiration. If you can better yourself, because of me, I think that's pretty good and it makes me feel good and it feels like maybe I'm doing something that's good. So that's where I'm at with my travels today.

It's interesting, I was kind of the black sheep of the family and that's cool today, because now I'm not. Somewhere along the way, I don't know when it happened, I went from being the black sheep to the star of the family. I won't say most popular, but definitely the most colorful. Even one of my nieces said, "Uncle Bean're, I'm glad we have you in our family, because if we didn't have you, our family would be boring." That was awesome. That made me feel really happy. So I would like to give back to them in some way. My nephew, he's playing guitar now. He's fourteen and I'd like to take him with me to some of the events. I've been trying to get him back stage at a few of the shows so he can meet these cats. His favorite band is AC/DC. I know those guys and I know people in other bands too. I hope to get him in to meet some of his heroes.

I admire my family a lot. My mother and my little brother and my stepfather and my sister – I'm still real close with them. And like I said, I have nieces and nephews and great nieces and nephews and I'd like to be able to bring them along on a little bit of this ride. They're reading this book now and they're watching me from afar.

Sometimes people ask me about the future, what do I have planned, do I have anything planned? I always tell them that instead of making some giant goal or fantasy destination, nothing can be as good as what could happen if I let it.

Having said that, I do have a few directions that I would like to take and one is Reality TV. I would like to get on a TV show and be watched by millions. I think that would be a good thing for several reasons. One being I could make even more of a difference in people's lives. You might notice that I do a lot of charity events and I like to help out. I don't have money. I can't start any sort of trust fund or endowment for a charity organization, but if I had some more notoriety, I could get more people behind me. It's no different than one person, like a movie star or a rock musician, endorsing something they believe in. Tweeting; one tweet about something and all of a sudden the media's attention is there and the people are jumping on that bandwagon and helping and that's a huge honor. It would be nice to say hey, everyone check this out and maybe some of you want to help, some of you don't, but just check it out. That is one thing I think that a stint on reality TV would enable me to do.

I could do what I do now, but just more. More travel, more people, more good impact on other people's lives.

People ask me, "What's your next plan?" I always say, it's the one I'm getting ready to start tomorrow - and I don't know what it is. But tomorrow's a new day and anything's possible. I'm just going to open myself up to what happens. I got a feeling that it's not over yet. I have more and more things happening every day and people calling me and I'm bumping into other people.

All the things that are happening to me wouldn't be happening if it wasn't for a good reason. So I continue the quest, keeping my eyes open all the time to what life is throwing at me. Whatever it is, I got a feeling it's going to be good and that could be book number two.

TIMOTHY REMUS

NINE PART 1

TOUR OF EUROPE AND MOROCCO
BY NERISSE TROMBETTA

The idea of riding Bean're's 1997 Harley Davidson Road King through Europe actually began several years ago. In the spring of 2001 he and I talked briefly about taking a ride somewhere and he offered to pick me up in Newark, New Jersey, at the airport. He would ride up from the bike rally at Myrtle Beach and from Newark we would head to Canada. He would drop me off in New York four days later. I was ready to go. It was a wonderful whirlwind trip of over 1600 miles to Nova Scotia, Prince Edward Island and New Brunswick, as well as 7 states in the U.S. We had a great time. It was the best trip I had ever taken, up till then.

Back in Miami, we talked about another trip and I suggested Europe, remembering his desire to go. He considered the idea, and the whole trip mushroomed from there. We finally agreed to go for three weeks beginning with the last week of August.

I began the agonizing job of finding out who could ship the bike. It soon became clear that shipping it on a boat was really cheap but not an option because the shippers would have to keep the bike for over 2 weeks prior to even getting it in a container for the journey. Then I started calling airlines, beginning with Lufthansa. When I heard that one way was $2600.00, I realized that we would have to compromise. So I went to the other end of the spectrum and called Alitalia. We had a great conversation and it went on for an hour but when I hung up I was no closer to getting any pertinent information or a price than when I started. Eventually I found Warren Transport in Tamarac, Florida, a company that actually organizes tours of Europe on motorcycles. They connected me with Angel at M & M

Worldwide, a transport company. He knew all the ins and outs immediately and said he could put the bike on Lauda Airlines to Munich or Vienna for $850, plus document preparation charges. They only needed the bike for 2 days prior to departure for U.S. Customs to run a stolen vehicle search.

My travel agent booked seats for us on the same Lauda Air flight and suddenly we were scheduled to leave on Thursday, August twenty third and return on Friday, September 14th and it all seemed so easy.

Now I began researching. I bought travel books: Europe Travel Book, Europe's Greatest Driving Tours, Camping Europe, Adventure Motorcycling and six of Rick Steve's Tour Guides, including France, Great Britain, Italy, Switzerland, Greece, Germany and Morocco, I read them every night and highlighted relevant paragraphs, or what I assume could be relevant paragraphs. And I spent hours and hours on the internet, reading about other peoples' trips, suggestions and ideas. I bought the suggested maps and pinned them up on the wall.

Bean're walks in, checks out the map, looks up distances between cities and says this is going to be great and that is it. Somewhere about now I should have stopped buying and reading tour books, but I am doing my thing. Too much reading leads to hours and hours on the phone talking to over a dozen different people in 3 countries about purchasing a carnet, the equivalent of a passport for the motorcycle. No one knows much of anything, but I finally discover that we don't need one for the countries we are visiting.

Then I begin the insurance phone calls, which continue forever, until I find Bergland Insurance in Phoenix, Arizona. Although we are only required to have liability, we opt to buy comprehensive insurance for the bike for one month, another $750. This will be worth the money just so I can sleep at night. The international driver's license is really simple, 5 minutes at AAA and $30, and we each have one. Mine is the equivalent of mad money. If this doesn't work out I can rent a car and escape.

Bean're has spent his time putting a new motor in the bike, a Rev Tech engine which is 100 cubic inches. It looks and sounds great. He also added mufflers to the exhaust pipes so the bike would be quieter and we would blend in better. Then he decided to have it painted and chose a deep sparkly purple with unbelievable metallic chips that shine with wild colors in the sun. So the bike is looking and sounding wonderful and ready to transport us in style, everywhere. At this point he has ridden this bike over 75,000 miles in less than 3 years, all pleasure miles. I have ridden on the back for 1600 miles.

Time is going by fast. He picks up a metal shipping pallet from a Harley dealer and he is off to M and M Worldwide. It is a frustrating and lengthy process. They want it to be empty of gas which is easy, the gas gauge shows empty unless you turn on the ignition. They want everything disconnected so it can't run, also easy for the same reason. There are a myriad of documents that they fill out and he has to sign and he needs originals and copies of the title, (in his case two titles, one for the bike and one for the custom engine), copies of his registration and drivers license, airline ticket and passport. Everything seems to be done, finally.

Then the next day Angel calls to say that U.S. customs has made a mistake, now that is a surprise. They need an original document so the shipping of the bike is delayed and will not be on the flight with us. I do not tell Bean're that Lauda Air doesn't fly on Sunday or Monday. So if customs doesn't clear the bike for Saturday's flight, we will have to wait till Tuesday. No use in having both of us worrying about it.

Packing clothes is torturous. I have to be very conservative and yet consider everything from the Swiss alps to Morocco. I finally decide to limit myself to two pairs of black jeans, leather pants, two long sleeve black T shirts, my beautiful leather jacket, hiking boots and my leather cowboy boots plus a pair of sandals, which I wear, a leather mini-skirt for fun, plus several sleeveless T shirts which can also be layered under other stuff when I am cold.

Everything is black so I can wear it forever. My leather gloves and 3 pair of socks also go in the duffle bag. I am sure that Beans has spent 5 minutes packing, but then he probably won't remember to bring shampoo.

THE GRAND EUROPEAN TOUR BEGINS

We have talked, imagined and dreamed and now our trip of a lifetime is beginning on August 23, 2001. Notice that the word planned is not mentioned. The only plan is to ride wherever we want and the weather allows, covering as many countries and enjoying everything as much as we can in three weeks.

Our incredible odyssey begins with a 10 hour flight on Lauda, a small Austrian Airline that flies to and from the USA five times a week. It is full and cramped, but shows 5 movies which we watch and watch and watch, very hypnotic.

I think I may have slept a total of 20 minutes. But it is as good as it can be unless we flew first class for $7,000 each! Both meals are very good and breakfast is very welcome.

Beans takes over in Munich airport and learns the monetary system immediately and the train system just as quickly and negotiates it all with ease while I sit and watch the mountain of luggage.

We are off to downtown Munich. Naturally the train is super clean, well designed, very organized and has great upholstery - we are in Germany! The subway ticket is good for 24 hours and nobody ever looks at it. Leave it to the Germans to have an honor system for the subway. It is early in the morning, we are lugging heavy luggage and have no idea where we are going. I would have opted for a taxi and Beans opts for learning the subway system, much more economical. This pattern is repeated over and over throughout the trip.

We finally find a small hotel, The Luitpold, with one vacancy, a few blocks from the central train station. Our suite is on the top floor and the maid is still cleaning. Struggling in our own way with jet lag, one of us is asleep as soon as the maid makes the bed, even though she is still vacuuming. And the other one is out shopping. Imagine that? And shopping isn't easy in Germany, all those lederhosen, ruffled blouses and tiered skirts. There is a beautiful fountain in a center square and beyond is the old city, which looks intriguing, but three McDonalds in three blocks plus a Burger King? When I get back with a snack and drinks Beans gets up long enough to eat a little and then we both sleep before dinner and a walk. Strolling through old town, which is very pretty and charming, we find an interesting restaurant where Beans falls in love with Weiner Schnitzel and we stuff ourselves.

After dinner he introduces me to the art of postcard buying and sending. He has made a new address book just for this trip with the name of everyone he knows. He is always surprising me. I have no addresses and am searching my memory and notebook! It is fun. Postcard score; Beans 25, Nerisse 3. We stroll through the side streets and discover the "nudie" bars, lots of them, but we are looking for a place where we can sit inside and he can smoke his afterdinner cigar. Finally we find a small beer bar. There is lots of teasing about Beans sneaking out in the middle of the night to catch the naked-dancing-girls-shows. "I didn't know I had to sneak!" And he does "sneak out" ostensibly to get pizza?

It is time to pick up the bike and we are both ready. We went out yesterday and did a dry run, making all the wrong turns and went to all the wrong cargo places so today should be easy. I am adjusted to the time change, but sleep deprived and very teary. It now seems like a good thing that the bike was delayed a day as we have had time to sleep and adjust to the time zone somewhat.

We pile everything onto the subway train and head off again. The process of getting the bike through customs is pretty simple, it just involves a lot of walking and paperwork. The first thing they ask him for is proof of liability insurance. It all seems slow, especially on Saturday when hardly anyone is working. Then they bring the motorcycle out on its metal pallet, with a fork lift. It looks so beautiful, shiny and purple with its new paint job, full of promise and adventure. A wonderful piece of familiarity, and I am happier already.

By 1:30 P.M. Beans has somehow packed everything on the bike. We each have an unwieldy duffle bag, one of us has a really messy big one and it isn't me!, and a third big duffle bag holds his tent, air mattress, tarp and air pump plus we each have a sleeping bag (guess who has the very tidy and smallest and who has the big one with a built in pillow which only cost $19.95?) The saddle bags are already full of maps, travel information books, tools, hiking boots, rain slickers and various other stuff. One duffle bag fits into the tour box on the back of the bike and the other 2 go on top, behind me. The sleeping bags are strapped on top of the saddlebags. They then create perfect holders for my water and/or soda bottles. We are quite top heavy and unwieldy but with extra bungee cords, Beans can use his side mirrors!

And we begin our adventure! A few turns out of cargo and we are on the autobahn and zipping along at 120 MPH. As soon as I am on the back of the bike, I feel wonderful. The ride is everything. As we take off, Beans says Happy Birthday! Today is my birthday. We are riding north towards Hamburg and the Danish border, Sweden and Norway. Totally the opposite of what I had expected. All the books that I spent months reading, and carefully editing; ripping out pages and chapters to save space and weight and then organized in ziplock bags by country, of possible destinations and sights, etc. there is nothing on Scandinavia. This should not have been a surprise. Beans has begun our completely freeform trip with no agenda and no schedule! I trust his judgments and decisions, implicitly, it just took a few hours for me to remember that.

Germany is very neat and very organized, but the countryside is not very exciting. Modern windmills seem to be everywhere, tall and white in the sedate landscape of extraordinarily neat and perfect farms. No rusting cars or abandoned bathtubs in the yards. In some areas they have built a framework of high wood poles in a tent shape with vines growing up the poles. Possibly to shade the crops underneath? The only billboards are very small McDonald signs, sitting on wheels in farmer's fields. Everyone drives perfectly, no one is going slow in the left lane or even stays in the left lane after passing. Everyone is predictable and very orderly. The signage is perfect and very understandable. A circle with three black diagonal lines through it = no speed limit. Beans loves the autobahn, the speed and the German drivers. "Enjoy it while you can, it won't last."

The weather is beautiful, but hot, we are riding in T shirts. German bikers are in complete leather or expensive fabric suits. Outside Magdeberg I talk to a biker in a Florida Marlins T shirt at a gas station along A19. We are stopping for gas a lot because of the weight and our high speed on the autobahn, but the gas stations are great with super bathrooms. However, fuel costs almost twice as much, but is better than American gas. Regular gas has an octane level of about 94 to 95 while super has an octane of 98 or above.

Beans is sure there must be a bike meet somewhere nearby as we are seeing so many motorcycles. He talks to a woman at a gas station and discovers there is a bike rally and not too far away. "Hurry, we have to go," and we race the setting sun to find it in Malchow, a very tiny charming town, not even on the map. We get there barely in time to put up our tent, just before it is totally dark, on a small patch of bare ground among 5000 motorcycles and their German riders. We decide to skip blowing up the air mattress so we won't miss anything. We will sleep on the unforgiving hard ground. Beans: "A biker rally for your birthday!" This is great and completely unexpected, which makes it even better.

Beans has negotiated the entry fee and gets us a deal. We are very low on German Marks as we were almost out of Germany and after much discussion and the usual gestures they finally agree to let us in for less, and then the negotiations start over because we have no money to buy tickets to get food and drink! The rock band is Vicky Vomit, The steaks are 87 cents US and taste great.

My birthday dinner is wonderful. We talk to several bikers there and are surprised to learn that they are very impressed by the scope and length of our trip. They have never ridden outside of Germany. We can not imagine why they aren't riding all over Europe all the time, since so many countries are so close by.

Then the women begin to notice Beans. He stands out, as usual, so very cool looking, tall, thin and with his long blond hair and tattoos, he is not blending in. They are all over him, pulling his ponytail etc. He's happy, lost nothing in translation. "It is all the same, but in German."

Next morning - somehow I actually slept through all the ever increasing racket of celebrating, drunk Germans and the rock band and guys chanting and pounding their feet for hours and hours. First recognizable German "Dumkopf" yelled at the chanters early this A.M. We walk and take pictures of the bikes, the guys are all waving at me, guess I really look American. Then we are back on the autobahn heading north.

GERMANY

Tall pine trees with orange trunks? Sunshine. Danka. Glass sound barriers along the autobahn to show off the best views. Yogurt on cereal. Polizicia. Brats and sauerkraut. Bridge abutments designed with lattice, vines, brickwork, fake doors etc. Very intricate and good graffiti everywhere. Cushmans on the autobahn? Who is sneaking out in the middle of the night?

Our first ferry takes us to Denmark and a fast drive past old windmills and pretty farms. Traffic backs up really badly because of a horrible roll over. Beans decides to test the passing laws of Denmark and does a great job of getting us out of the mess, mostly on the shoulder combined with a lot of weaving in and out among motionless cars, on the autobahn. The back-up goes on and on for miles, oops kilometers. After getting past the unbelievable accident, we meet up with a red Ferrari, the road opens up and the car takes off. Beans stays right with him even with the heavy load and the restrictive exhaust pipes. The Ferrari goes no faster than 120 MPH and when the road dead ends at a ferry port we are still right behind him. The driver stops and immediately pops the hood to look over his motor, something must be wrong if a Harley Davidson is keeping up without a problem. Our second Ferry ride is to Sweden, a quick 45 minutes. Love these ferries.

RIDE RIDE RIDE

Through Sweden Beans is looking for the girl's volleyball team! The country is getting prettier all the time, but no team. We decide to camp and Beans finds a place south of Halmstead, that is very, very, neat and clean. As soon as the tent and air mattress are ready Beans is stretched out and asleep before sunset. It's been a long day. I take pictures as the sun sets.

Then the dew arrives, very heavy dew and everything is getting soaking wet very quickly. In the process of trying to get it all in the tent I wake Beans. We decide to head down the road to the recommended pizza place. Very weird dinner, definitely should have had pizza. My "lamb kabobs" turn out to be very thinly sliced mystery meat but served with delicious pommes frittes. (French fries to us Yanks.) Beans has pasta, very Chef Boyardee. Anyway we did eat and rode a short distance to see the lights on the shoreline. It is cold.

The camping was great until the wind got wild in the middle of the night and my sleeping bag and air mattress were rising and falling unpredictably with the tent floor and then the rain started and 100% of me got really wet sleeping in a puddle.

I didn't realize how cold and wet I was until I got up and started shaking. But the bathrooms are fantastic: a card to get 4 minutes in a very hot shower and a large sign asking you to take off your shoes before entering the shower!? The toilets have a choice of large or small flush! The many windows each have embroidered white cafe curtains. And along the walkways are perfectly manicured little flower and vegetable gardens.

129

It is time to go again and he piles all the wet stuff back on the bike and we take off. Not too far north a semi pulls up alongside of us and signals that we have lost some luggage. The bag with the tent is gone. After some rather rough language, Beans leaves me on the side of the road and heads off the wrong way on the emergency lane of the autobahn to, hopefully, find the duffle bag. And there it is in the middle of the highway about two miles back and, miraculously, no one has driven over it! Our first little mishap, but all is well. A little reworking with the bungees and we are off again, heading for Norway.

The scenery keeps getting better and better and suddenly we are crossing a bridge linking Sweden and Norway and Oh My God! What an incredible fjord. It is astonishingly deep, steep and beautiful on both sides. Beans, who never stops, immediately pulls over and digs out his camera. I have already done several hold-my-hand-up-as-high-as-possible-and-point-and shoot pictures, as we zoom over the bridge. When we stop for the good shots my battery dies, very predictable. We dodge speeding semis and go back and forth across the bridge to get shots with his camera from both sides. Then a stop at the tourist Information Booth, where Beans loads up on postcards and ferry information and I use the ATM to get Norwegian Kroner (or is it crouton?), and we are off to Oslo. Now I am taking pictures one after the other, as if after the next bend in the road it will all be over and become flat and uninspiring. But it never stops. What a beautiful country. I am so glad that my tour guide insisted on going North, he is the best!

As we approach Oslo there is a toll booth, Beans decides to run it and is exhilarated that he broke the law. By the second toll booth he discovers a sign: "motorcycles gratis." They even have a special lane just for motorcycles to zip through without paying. "Abonnemont" becomes the word as we fly through toll booths.

Everything was packed wet so we opt for a hotel. The first place we try acts like we are invisible so we walk out. At the second one everyone is super nice and offer: "You can park your bike in the laundry area where it will be safe, although it is totally against the rules." The room has gorgeous wood floors, doors and furniture and a beautiful bath with tub which Beans enjoys. I spread wet sleeping bags over the beautiful doors. We clean up and go out for a stroll looking for dinner while Beans enjoys the sights.

We finally decide on The Eden for dinner after a long walk and reading many menus. There are lots of bikes parked out front, a good sign, and the bikers are sitting at tables outside, but because it is too cold for us, we opt for inside. The steaks are great, and after dinner we have drinks outdoors and he enjoys a cigar. We are sitting across from a pretty park and it is all very idyllic. A leisurely stroll back to the hotel and now he is hungry again. Beans is busy disarming and charming everyone and making friends everywhere. The bartender is ready to give him anything he wants, but she doesn't have a dessert he likes, so he settles on lobster soup to take to the room. And more postcards. He is going to have to join postcards anonymous.

A great free breakfast with lots of wonderful cheeses and cold bologna and mortadella, cereal with yogurt and two kinds of herring! plus the US standard eggs and bacon. We eat and write postcards. Beans 28, Nerisse 6.

Time to load it all on the bike again. Now he is getting a crowd watching him outside the hotel. They look at the luggage piled high on the sidewalk and the bike and figure he will never be able to get all this stuff on there. But he does it again and we are off to look for the Harley dealer in Oslo. We want to buy shirts. It takes us forever to find this place, which is so hidden on a little alley-way in the middle of a residential area. Our last set of directions comes from a biker who is teaching a bike riding class and his students are trying to negotiate an obstacle course. So as we leave Beans has to give it a try and does an incredible job, especially with me on the back, plus our top-heavy load.

The Harley shop is disappointing so we quickly buy two shirts and are soon back on the road and heading for Kristiansand where we hope to catch a ferry. The ride is beautiful and we are racing the rain and win. Next discovery, Norwegian hot-dogs wrapped in bacon at the gas stations! Mmmmm! But we are too late for the ferry and so we take off, racing for Stavanger to see if we can get there in time for that ferry to Newcastle. It is a race where we don't even know the rules since we have no idea what time it is. As Beans says he really doesn't want to know since then he will try too hard. The roads are very curvy and we are regularly leaning in the turns so far that the floor boards are dragging. The weather is better and we can get rid of the slickers. At a gas station we finally ask the time and discover we have one and a half hours of riding left to get to Stavanger and only a half hour before the ferry leaves. "Are you sure we can't make it? Oh, well." We order more hot dogs and Fanta lemon sodas.

The Scandinavians are quite ingenious as they have designed their plastic bottle caps to remain attached to the bottles so there is no litter. We decide to take it easy and enjoy the ride as it just keeps getting better and better. We eat potato chips as we ride. I am feed-ing him a few at a time as they blow away! Every gas station has in-credible choices of four different types of hot dogs and we have gotten into the bad habit of filling both the gas tank and us. So we are religiously following Bean're's instructions; ride and eat. We are both amazed by the incredible, wild mountain views and peaceful, very little towns that we pass. The police follow us for a while and apparently decide to leave us alone.

We arrive in Stavanger and check into a hotel where they have a gated parking lot for the bike and go looking for dinner!!! In the morning it is another wonderful breakfast and then we pack, load the bike, in front of another crowd, and head for Bergen where we hope to catch a ferry to Aberdeen. This ride is even better than any-thing we have seen so far. Incredibly beautiful, we hope it goes on forever.

THE RIDE, THE RIDE, THE RIDE.

It is impossible to describe this ride from Stavenger to Bergen. We thought we had seen beautiful fjords and mountains, villages and the sea, but this is even more sensational. As Beans said, "Nothing can compare to this ride." The road is narrow and very twisting and turning, always climbing or descending and sometimes becoming too narrow for two large vehicles to get by. The ride includes two tunnels underwater, one a 9% grade road, 8 km long, going down under the water for miles before leveling off and then starting back up the other side, especially beautiful bridges and then twice the road ends and we board a ferry to cross the water and find the road on the other side. The little ferries are very charming and almost elegant. The last one had little pots of purple violets on the tables. And food, too, we seem to always be eating!

Every twist and turn of the road opens up a view that is breathtaking and overwhelmingly beautiful. Neither one of us can believe what we are seeing. It brings tears to my eyes, very emotional. We are touching floor boards on the turns and it is a dream of a ride until we round a curve and find a semi coming at us in our lane. There isn't even time for me to scream. Beans does an expert job of riding again and saves us from destruction. We never would have had room in even a tiny car to get by. There is no shoulder and no guard rails and the drop off is, as always, severe with sheer rock on the other side. There are many places where buses and semis wait for some unknown signal so that they can safely proceed.

From Stavenger to Bergen is 160 Km of incredible beauty, as Beans says "It just keeps coming at you." No end to the beauty and breathtaking views plus the little colorful wood houses, painted red, in perfect condition with perfect yards and farm land, perfect rock walled fields filled with grazing sheep, all clinging to the cliffs, facing spectacular views, with small fishing boats in the natural harbors.

Late in the day we pull into Bergen, a lovely town with old buildings built around a harbor and surrounded by mountains. We spend a lot of time trying to decipher the ferry schedules and where the different ferry companies are located.

The streets are very hilly and cobblestone, not a comfortable ride. At one point we are facing an extremely steep descent on a very narrow street with wet cobblestones and decide not to try it with this very top-heavy bike. Finally, we give up on trying to get a ferry out of here right away and get a hotel room. We will enjoy this beautiful town while we wait for the ferry to Newcastle that leaves on Thursday. Beans finds an apartment at the Ole Bull Eiendom since every hotel room in Bergen is full and it turns out to be very nice. Well, first they give us a key for a room and it is really tiny and comes with two people already in the bed, so after much laughter and apologies, we get a two room apartment, just completely redone, with a complete kitchen, on the top floor for the same money and Beans finds a spot under our window in a dead end alley for the bike. Perfect.

We head out to find a good dinner. Lots of exploring and walking on narrow hilly streets and we end up at a little restaurant on the waterfront at the harbor, on the central plaza. After a lot of menu discussion Beans orders whale and caribou, always pushing it over the edge! I have conventional seafood. And we share very fresh raw oysters and delicious lobster soup. And for dessert there are berries and creme fraiche. Sinfully good! We love our dinners. And walk to our home for two days, to watch TV: the weirdest Japanese game show dubbed in English with Norwegian subtitles! The movies are often in English, but have Norwegian subtitles, which our brains stubbornly keep trying to read, for some weird reason.

In the morning Beans does our laundry, surprising me again. It is a challenge, but they do have German machines which are fantastic at cleaning. Then we do the tourist thing and ride the cable car to the top of the mountain and enjoy a spectacular view in every direction.

Then we ride down to town again to have lunch. There are so many pretty little streets with charming and unique shops, great for window shopping. Our purchases are severely limited by lack of space on the bike. The large central plaza fills up with tables of vendors selling everything from fresh seafood to fruit; jewelry to reindeer skins and others that I won't mention. Norway is very complex: an incredibly beautiful country with wonderful people, but they are still killing whales and seals. Beans wants a reindeer skin and I am ignoring him.

As we ride around town, he waves at all the little kids who are entranced by the sight of us. They stare and grin and shyly wave. For dinner it is back to our favorite restaurant, Zachariasbrygge Seafood Bar, by the harbor. We both decide to order lobster. Beans goes inside to view the holding tank and make the decision; which ones go into the pot. I am going to remain outside at the table, blissfully unaware, sipping my wine. He has charmed the waitress, as usual, and she has brought us a free plate of shrimp, heaped high and delicious. This continues throughout the trip as we get little gifts or extras almost everywhere we go. The lobster arrives. They are absolutely huge and picture perfect. Four pounds each! And they are fantastically good. We savor every mouthful. But, unfortunately, it is more than either of us can eat.

It is time to get ready for our ferry ride on Fjord Line to Newcastle, England, across the North Sea. Beans loads everything on the bike in a misty rain. Somehow we are early so he grabs the opportunity and runs over and after much negotiation, buys a reindeer pelt which somehow he manages to strap on the back of the bike ... At least this addition looks good!

Now we just have to get up a rain slicked ramp made of steel mesh grating rising from the dock up several stories, with a sharp left turn right at the top, on a very overloaded bike ... Beans teases me and gets me nervous and then makes it look easy and I am relieved. Later a Scottish man on deck asks us if we saw those crazy people with that seriously overloaded bike, go up the ramp? Apparently the entire load of cars in line was watching us and didn't believe that we would make it. We were conversation again.

Our room is laughably small with no porthole. Only one of us can stand up at a time. Originally we went into the wrong room, which we thought was too small, but in retrospect the solution is either to stand in line to negotiate a bigger room or adapt. We adapt. Beans helps himself to the fruit from a first-class room, bringing it to our small cabin and we feel much better!! Oranges, bananas and pears. Very good. We race Saga cars video games and eat again and gamble on slots and lose. And watch Pearl Harbor in the movie theater. After dinner we share a cigar outside with great conversation and misty rocks and mountains going by as we leave Norway and head across the North Sea. We find that smoking cigars on the ships deck always guarantees us the use of a large part of the deck to ourselves, while everywhere else is crowded.

Beans creates a "wake" everywhere we go with his look. Somehow I am always two steps behind him and see the reaction as heads turn and people smile. He definitely does not blend in! I watch and enjoy.

A huge breakfast buffet separates the seasick from the non seasick. We, of course are going back for seconds and thirds. The ferry ride was pretty "bouncy" during the night, as the Scottish lady says, but we loved it. Really must have been rough seas though, as it tossed this huge loaded ferry around, but we didn't wake up enough to get it together and go out and look.

The ferry docks smoothly and soon we are riding down the ramp. Motorcycles on ferries are always loaded first and then usually get to leave first! An added bonus. Riding through the English countryside with the Beans, driving on the left. The roundabouts, traffic circles, are confusing, but he gets the hang of it immediately, as usual, and we have a beautiful ride from Tyne to the ferry in Kingston Upon Hull. Stop for McDonalds on the way and British pounds. Have we eaten McDs in every country so far?

"I'm going to get gas." "You wouldn't take off and leave me just because you have the cash and the credit card?" The bikers parked near us are very concerned as he takes off for the gas station, right next door, and I am walking. "Did he go off and leave you?," they ask.

It is sunny and beautiful, lots of old brick houses, bed and breakfasts and lovely pubs all with charming flower gardens and shutters along the way. We get to Hull early and find a shop to weld the air filter cover back on, so we are lookin' good again.

"We must have fish n' chips," says the Beans, so off to town we go. And on the central square we find the Golden Fry with a restaurant on the second floor. As Beans gets to the top of the stairs and turns to walk to the table, about six young girls working there start tittering, smiling and blushing and being shy. They are obviously very impressed by him!! And he is oblivious. I enjoy. He gets a table by the window so he can keep an eye on our gear and the bike. Everyone is checking out his motorcycle, including a Bobbie, an English police officer. Beans takes pictures of the unaware Bobbie from the second floor window. Meanwhile we enjoy a huge and delicious serving of fried fish and potatoes. Back down on the street, Beans enjoys a cigar resting on the bike. We walk on the square that is surrounded by gigantic lovely old buildings and in the center is a massive statue of Queen Victoria, and a little old lady feeding the pigeons. Every light pole has a basket overflowing with flowers hanging from fancy metal brackets.

Then we are off to P & 0 North Sea Ferries to ride to Rotterdam. Lots of motorcycles this time. We have learned our lesson and buy a first-class ticket so we have a larger stateroom with bunk beds and a view. Another overnight ferry. They are wonderful, as you cover miles and miles while you sleep and there is usually a mini movie theater. This time we watch Cats and Dogs and Planet of the Apes while sitting on the floor in front so we can stretch out our legs. What day is it? The popcorn is really bad, but dinner and breakfast are good.

As we arrive in Rotterdam, our sixth country, it is foggy and rainy, socked in, but beautiful still. We put on our rain gear hoping to intimidate the rain, but it doesn't work as well this time. Flowers are everywhere, window boxes brimming over, gardens loaded with vegetables, fields of blue green onion leaves, mounds of very colorful and huge squash for sale on the side of the road, little houses and their wonderful gardens close to the road and two James Bond Aston Martins. It is very cold and damp and, of course, all very flat with very wide canals everywhere.

We stop in a tiny town, Horn, Netherlands, for lunch. Local families come and have coffee and pie and motorcycle riders are having a beer out front. Very charming. Neither one of us can read Dutch and the menu is huge and we are getting nervous about ordering and getting something weird. The waiter doesn't speak any English at all. Just slightly better than our Dutch. We finally find goulash on the menu which is perfect since we are so cold and it is delicious. The Dutch menu makes a disaster a real possibility until I see wiener schnitzel on the third page and we are safe. It is delicious and comes with a salad and seven bowls of vegetables and potatoes. We stuff ourselves and then I have to order pie because it looks so good. Now that we have completely stuffed ourselves, can we stay awake on the bike! And the check arrives: I pull out my visa, "not possible, is broken", the waiter says. I offer to pay with US dollars? "not possible," pay with American Express checks "not possible." So Beans has to get directions and drive to the nearest bank/ATM and get Dutch money while I stay as hostage?

It is getting colder, but the rain seems to be over. We have used their spacious bathrooms to change into our long underwear, and leather pants for me. We ride into Brussels and suddenly the flat land gives way to hills and another kind of beauty. Each country has its own personality.

We arrive in Luxembourg and stop for gas at a real truck stop. There isn't even a ladies room at this gas station. It only has one large co-ed bathroom. Beans talks me into buying a "souvenir," a gigantic green plaid flannel shirt lined with imitation sheepskin. It is enormous, almost to my knees and the sleeves hang at least 8 inches beyond my fingertips. I am concerned about the price, having no idea the value of Luxembourg money. He finally convinces me when he points out that it costs the same as the tank of gas and, "We are going to ride late and you will need it to keep warm." My leather jacket looks great with lots of long fringe, buffalo bones and silver trim, but is short, small and not very warm.

Then through France where the hills give way to mountains. We can see the alps in the distance for a long time and then suddenly we are in the French alps and it is so beautiful. Once again we are surrounded by breathtaking scenery.

Once again the drive is incredible, through a tunnel 3300 meters and then we are tossed out onto a viaduct, two lanes in each direction on two different levels clinging to the sides of the mountain, and resting on huge concrete pilings so they appear to be rising above the mountain side. A sheer drop down as it twists and turns for miles and then plunges you into yet another long tunnel and continues to repeat itself over and over. I lose track of the number of tunnels. At the end I am becoming terrified of the curves, tunnels and bridges at hair-raising speeds. I try to talk myself out of being afraid and can't do it - a combination of being cold, hungry, tired and on insane roads. Beans tries to reassure me, but I am not buying it. We finally arrive in Geneva and find a hotel after 13 + hours of riding, 750 miles and five countries! The interesting thing is that once you have been riding for six hours or so you are in a zone and then even at 13 hours you feel like you can continue to sit here and go forever. Of course all I have to do is sit! Bean're has an incredible ability to sit perfectly still and just keep going and going, no matter what the challenges are. He seldom even stretches his legs out onto the crash bars.

The moon is full and rising over the alps as we arrive at the Mercure Hotel, with that totally wild look you can only achieve after hours on a motorcycle, and in my case complicated by the worst helmet hair. Beans has the wild and woolly motorcycle mustache. But they welcome us, anyway and give us a large and wonderful room. It is after 9:00 P.M. and the restaurant is already closed, but they offer to let us order dinner and they will send it up to our room, so we can eat in bed! A perfect solution for us, as we are starved but very tired. Dinner is three lamb chops for me with a liter of wine and filet mignon with ham encrote and two alcohol-free beers for Beans. The people are lovely. Switzerland is spectacular. And we are both exhilarated and exhausted.

Up again at 7:00 A.M. to start our ride to Zermatt. There seems to be a slight cloud of smoke behind us now, which is a concern. There is a discussion about what could be causing this, but there is not much that can be done at this point, so we continue. Beans is anxious to get to the Matterhorn and snow board. The road zig zags back into France which is perfect since we find a Brasserie and stop for a great French breakfast, my favorite, at Le Grillandain in Chamonix, a small town that is unbelievably picturesque, near Mont Blanc. We are wearing our long underwear and everything else we can and the village natives are walking around in shorts. It is cold, miserable and raining and we pass a guy walking, in shorts without a shirt. A man and a little boy in shorts and T shirts with their dog who at least had a long shaggy coat, the only one sensibly dressed in that group. This is their summer!

As we ride towards Mount Blanc we look up and suddenly, there is snow on the mountain tops, shining in the sun. And I think I see people skiing. Very exciting, especially for someone who wants to snow board! And then parasailers suddenly appear over the top of one of the highest mountains and their colorful chutes slowly descend towards the valleys so very far below. That is beyond brave!

The scenery is incredible and the first road we take to Martingy, Switzerland is narrow, full of literal hairpin curves and lots of exciting twists and turns and more tunnels and bridges. As the brochure says, the most expensive roads per mile to build in the world. The signs on the roads are not as good. The arrow indicating a curve does not indicate the actual direction that the road will take and the direction signs for approaching towns are sporadic and undependable. We are moving fast and enjoying every moment, though. Arrive in Tasch at noon and get a room with a balcony at the Alpen Hotel where we can actually lie in bed and see the massive Matterhorn outside our window. Beans rushes to change into his snow boarding clothes. He looks great. We dash across the street to the train station, load up on Swiss chocolate bars, postcards and newspapers and jump on the train to Zermatt. After a long walk through town to the cable cars, we find out that they won't let anyone ski after 1:00 P.M. because the sun is too warm on the snow. We decide to check out the mountain top anyway and take the three lifts to the top. After one gondola and two cable cars, we walk through a long tunnel and out onto the mountain. It is amazing. We think we are at the top, but later discover an elevator and a series of metal stairs that really go to the top.

It is a perfectly clear day and the view is forever. We are over 13,000 feet high and the glacier looks wet and full of huge, dangerous crevasses. It is very windy and cold, but sunny and clear so the views are spectacular; all the peaks that surround us, including the Matterhorn and the huge valley leading down to Zermatt, Tasch and beyond. A Japanese couple takes our picture at the top. Beans gives me his sweatshirt which is toasty and big enough to fit over my jacket. We stop in a small hut at the top for hot chocolate and talk with a British man who has abandoned his climb up Breithorn Mountain, 4160 meters, with his two children. The little girl isn't four years old yet! Apparently their feet got too cold to continue. The rest of the family is still climbing. They are a different breed of people here! But then he might say the same thing about us riding on our bike across Europe.

There are crowds of skiers and snow boarders leaving the mountain in a rush, few going up. Everyone returning looks exhausted and very flushed with that clear mountain-air skin. Lots of climbers in the cars on the way down, interesting, lean and quite serious, eating meats and brie. One appears to be the hiking equivalent of the ski bum. The Swiss are so efficient that when the cable cars are stopped at the platforms, the sparrows come out from underneath the station to clean out the crumbs left by snacking skiers and hikers.

Back in Tasch, Bean're gets out his tools and takes a look at the motor to try and determine the cause of the smoke. He checks the valves and push rods for proper alignment. Removes the compression release buttons and checks for leaks and replaces the spark plugs. Everything seems to be in order except that the plugs are wet with oil. Not a good sign. Pizza for dinner and early to bed since he will be up before 7:00 A.M. to catch the train to Zermatt.

SEPTEMBER 4, TUESDAY

It is raining and therefore probably snowing at the top, Beans is gone long before 7:00 to the train station in the rain. I nap a little and watch the weather in German, It is raining everywhere in Europe except southern Italy. Good day to be here. Shower and wash some clothes, which I drape over the light fixture in the bathroom to dry. Nothing if not inventive. Off to Zermatt and the cable cars to the top to try to photograph Beans, but it is like a mini blizzard that only occasionally blows open so I can see one slope and dozens of mini skiers. I take pictures anyway when the snow curtain blows open; one of those tiny dots down there is probably him. I ride down the mountain with various ski team members in beautiful ski clothes each carrying several sets of skies and an auger to set their slalom poles.

Beans is back. He snow boarded for over six hours and says it was fun, but exhausting at over 13,000 feet, with only short trails open and only T bars for lifts. It snowed most of the time and his first run was untouched powder, the best. The ski team from Switzerland was practicing and invited him to snow board down their slalom course. Very cool. And he did the famous run to Cervinia, Italy and had lunch there. He beat me to Italy.

We pack a box and ship it to the States to lighten the load, getting rid of the reindeer pelt, all the snow board stuff and various odds and ends. But it hasn't made much of a dent in the luggage we are carrying.

We pack our duffle bags again and Beans loads the bike before another very large crowd. They are fascinated and applaud us as we ride off, full of smiles. When we first start there isn't any smoke, so we look good and we want to believe that it fixed itself! But once the bike warms up the smoke starts getting bad.

The ride out is as adventurous as the ride in. Several signs indicate 12% grades, which Beans loves. The mountain rides bring out the best in him; lots of challenges and he is fantastic at meeting each one. Anyone else would have given up, been in a crash or opted for a less demanding drive way before now. We fly up and down the winding road through the Alps to Italy and the Autostrada. We slow down as we approach the border but immigration officers smile and wave us through as we leave our smoke trail. We are never stopped at any border so the stamps we had hoped to collect in our passports are almost non-existent.

We leave Switzerland where everything is orderly and neat and tidy and everyone drives perfectly, and cross the border and everything is in ruins, old and tumbling and romantic and everyone drives like they are totally mad. I love it!

ITALY

Horrible cigars. A girl on a bright red bicycle with red shoes, red purse, red T shirt, red pants, red jacket and red hat. Grazie. How can there be no tortellini in Italy? McDrive. Espresso and Frosties. Insanely aggressive drivers. Wonderful Italian street names. Statues, huge and ornate, everywhere. Serious security. Italy is wonderful.

Italy begins with a series of small villages filled with very old buildings in various stages of disrepair, full of charm. And then an amazing ride through tunnels one after the other. Long dark tunnels that open to sunlight for only half a minute or less and then you are back in another long tunnel curving through the mountains around Lake Como. They seem to be endless. We have spent a lot of our drive going through tunnels in Norway, then France, Switzerland and now Italy. I should have kept a count.

Originally, the only real plan we had was that we would skip the big cities and enjoy the small towns and countryside that as a tourist we would not normally see. It would be an exceptionally unusual experience. But because of the problems with the bike we will be going into the big cities to see if we can get someone to repair it or the parts for Bean're to fix it.

Milano: they drive like insane people, but Beans adapts immediately. The first stop light he is complaining about all the cars that are suddenly sharing his lane and the motorcycles weaving past our knees to get to the front of the line, and by the second light he is right there with them, which is the only way. They turn two lanes into four and they park everywhere. Two rows of angle parking, the second row on the sidewalks. Parking where it clearly states no parking. Motorcycles are often ridden on the sidewalks. The laws are made to be broken. Beans has adapted so well that he is already going the wrong way on one-way streets.

We stop for gas on the outskirts of Milan and to access the burning oil situation which has become very bad. The smoke is so thick now that at the toll booths they are closing the window to protect themselves and waving their hands. The Italian police, at a road block after a toll booth, look like they are pulling us over and then change their mind. We are both very concerned and hope to find a Harley mechanic in Milan. The gas station attendant speaks no English but finds a Harley dealer in the phone book for us. We buy a quart of oil for 16,000 Lire! and we are off heading for the center of the city through the insane traffic.

144

Beans finds the Hotel Piemonte, a small hotel with gated parking although by now he is hoping someone will steal the bike! Our small room has pink marble floors, an Italian bathroom with a bidet and through a 12 foot glass door, a huge tiled balcony. The view is of postage stamp yards, walled and gated and very landscaped, hidden behind "brownstones." The TVs get smaller with each room and it is all in Italian now, a real challenge. The elevators are getting smaller too. I walk up the curving marble stairs because we both can't fit in with our luggage. We stagger out to find dinner and find a nice small pasta place, after a long walk and lots of grumbling. We are both tired. Beans wanted food delivered, but they don't even understand the concept at the front desk. And also no tortellini, which upsets him. But this restaurant has a delicious cold antipasti buffet and our pasta is wonderful. There is a deaf couple in the corner talking in sign language. Italians using sign language!

In the morning the charming breakfast is in a beautiful tiny room alongside the lobby and includes delicious cappuccino, espresso, rolls and Frosties! Off to find the Harley shop. Beans is the master at deciphering impossible streets, (the names literally change every other block) while negotiating impossible traffic, insane drivers, huge roundabouts, reading a map and always knowing where he is. It is wild, but somehow he keeps it all together and makes it look easy. If he dropped me off now I wouldn't even be able to get back to the hotel by taxi. The first shop isn't open and so we wait out front.

We buy T shirts at the first Harley dealer and get directions to Numero Uno HD and once again Beans finds this tiny alley and the shop, a cluster of three buildings. There is much conversation and parts books come out and more conversation and they finally decide they can't work on a custom engine. On to a third dealer, where they finally say they can fix a Rev Tech motor, but it will take a week, which in Italian translates to 3 weeks, if everything goes smoothly. So that will not work and we are faced with an even more difficult decision. To give up, to push the bike and see what happens, to find somewhere to buy the parts and Beans can repair it, or?

It is overwhelmingly sad. Beans finally decides to keep going and see how it goes. So we pack up again and are off towards Florence, Tuscany and Abruzzi. I can not believe how Beans adapted and drove like a true Italian. He went to three Harley shops, back to the hotel and got on the Autostrada with barely a hitch. He is amazing as usual, "You ain't seen it all yet." That's what I am hoping.

About the time I have dredged up three or four remembered phrases in a language for the country we are leaving I am starting over. Except for Norway where I never learned any words at all. Most of the time I am saying thank you in French to Italians or vice versa. Beans sticks with his French, which is not very good, but the best of our foreign language knowledge.

South of Milano the land is flat again, with mountains off in the distance. The farms are like estates with beautiful old two-story buildings all clustered together in various stages of disrepair, seemingly connected and added on to as the decades passed. There are huge charming buildings with two story arches filled with stacks of drying hay. And all in the color I love, that muted and multi shaded terra cotta. The scenery is different than anything we have seen and it is wonderful. Lunch is at McDonalds, again. I think we need something familiar, easy and comforting, without a challenge to be met or a decision to mull over. "Number three, please." Beans orders, holding up three fingers. How can anyone mess up an order off a McDonalds value meal menu? Almost every time we try they cannot translate three fingers held up.

A couple approaches Beans to ask directions! He does look like he knows what he is doing!

We are almost to Florence when we reassess the situation with the smoking purple monster. The smoke is awful and who knows where it might finally stop running altogether. Beans is pretty sure that a broken ring is causing the problem. We look at a map and decide to head for Genoa where we can, hopefully ship the bike back to the U.S. It is a very tough decision but we are making the only choice. Every once in awhile we think that it has stopped smoking or maybe it is smoking less. It is only wishful thinking. We are both very sad and quiet. I am only 45 minutes from Tuscany, which, in the beginning was number one on my list. My original thought was to ride down the east coast of Italy to Brindisi, catch a ferry to Corfu in Greece and then return through Tuscany and up the west coast of Italy. But we have to change course and head to Genoa.

Ahead of us still lies the spectacular Cinque Terre, along the west coast. It is more mountains and these are monstrous, soft and fat looking, completely covered with trees and very green. Suddenly in between two monster green hills is a little town with several beautiful church steeples piercing the sky, all set in a narrow valley opening out to an incredibly blue Mediterranean Sea. Actually it is Mer Ligure. More curving and more insane roads. Up, down and around, plus the crazy Italians driving. So many picturesque little towns on the mountain sides. And then my camera battery dies again. I have been taking a lot of pictures!

It is very bittersweet as we are enjoying this beautiful ride, but knowing it is coming to an end. There is still nothing like the ride. It makes everything better and anything worth the effort. Nothing is better than riding on a motorcycle and especially through the countries we have been lucky enough to enjoy.

Just a few miles south of Genoa and we see a camp ground up a tiny steep road and we decide to stop. A girl comes to the entrance to check us in, very beautiful, young and very Italian. (Unshaved underarms ... That's the look I have been striving for all this time!) Lots of gestures and broken English and we finally agree to pitch our tent on gravel, but overlooking the mountainside, if we remove the green cloth on the cyclone fence blocking our view and the breeze, which we do. We tie it up with some bungee cords.

Then we remember dinner. The girl assures us there is no restaurant anywhere nearby but she can order pizza for us, and they deliver. Unimaginable, but perfect. There is our usual banter and laughter setting up the tent and blowing up the air mattress, my job, with Beans to finish when it gets to the "hard part."

These bathrooms are different. The row of toilets offer two options, depicted on the stall doors. #1 is the familiar toilet and #2 is a hole in the ground with assigned places for your feet. Neither option has toilet paper, but a funky sprayer, hooked on the wall. Then we are off to the doccia. A coed row of very tiny cubicles where the first challenge is to figure out where to put your clothes so they well be relatively dry after the shower. It is very bizarre. The Italian men are talking loudly, I feel like they are in this tiny stall with me.

I am barely out of the shower when Beans comes to tell me the pizza has arrived! His Pepperoni translated to pepperoncini, which are red and green peppers, but there are two pizzas, very large and very delicious. We eat overlooking the pool and the beautiful mountain side as the sun sets.

Although we are very upset about having to send the bike back we both realize that nobody we know would have made it this far. We have ridden over 3000 miles in 11 days, including two days when we never went anywhere, and excluding ferry rides. Our longest day was 750 miles in just over 13 hours. We have traveled through 11 countries. We rode North almost to the arctic circle and South to the center of Italy. From 12,900' in the Alps to below sea level in Norway. We have negotiated Marks, Kroner, Pounds, Gilders, Francs and Lire. As Beans says, "Anyone else would have crashed, gotten sick, given up or been too scared or tired to continue." We have done exceptionally well and it has been a hell of a ride! An incredible trip. We laugh and relax and he enjoys a cigar. In the tent we are laughing and comparing sleeping bags, "I have this great built-in pillow." "I can unzip the foot and stick my feet out!" "Mine cost only $19.95! How much did you pay for yours?" "Never mind! But I can stuff mine into a smaller bag than yours!"

It seems that as soon as we slide into the sleeping bags, the noise intensifies. We have, and not in order of annoyance: kids crying, parents yelling at them to go to bed - this started before we ate the pizza and is seemingly unending - motorcycles and trucks downshifting and racing up and down the road, church bells and, of course, the dogs barking, and it is all echoing through the mountains. If that isn't enough, not one but two bright vapor lights come on right over our tent at dusk, just after Beans says, "It is going to get really dark." And all night, while trying to ignore this cacophony of unending noise, I know the roosters are coming and they do not disappoint us. But once again I prove that I can sleep through almost anything.

Morning finally comes and after a lack of good sleep and facing tough decisions and our last ride, we are very subdued and silent, the opposite of last night's laughter, fun and positive outlook. Mornings are the toughest.

All too soon we are out of the beautiful mountains and in Genoa. We go straight to the port, as Beans wants to find a shipping company as soon as possible. He picks one at random. Several minutes later he comes out and says they can ship it and seem to really want to ship it for him. One for one. Now to find a hotel, hopefully near by. Much tougher, as the first three we try are full and the forth is up a very narrow pedestrian alleyway in what could be the worst section of this city. They are too excited that he wants a room! A lady from a neighboring shop comes out to warn me about the area. Beans hates riding this smoking bike anywhere and is frustrated and tired, but he perseveres until we find a place that has a vacancy and where I will be able to walk outside without being mugged: The Star President. It is far from the port but across the street from the train station. And there is a bellhop. A very welcome innovation. I do laundry in the sink and hang it under the halogen lights to dry where it is nice and hot.

Dinner is at the Piedgrotta, a charming restaurant slightly below sidewalk level where we sit by the street, but inside. The waiter is charming. When in doubt fortify yourself with food. A promise of tortellini for Beans. Then the waiter comes back he is very sorry but

149

they are out of tortellini! So we order salads and pastas and speidini for a mere 78,500 Lire! Ah, the Italians are wonderful. We stroll along the park on our way home.

The negotiations with Masini Transporti Depositi of Genoa continue slowly and we are very depressed. Even though we are comforting ourselves with a fancy hotel and room service. Beans doesn't want to ride this bike anymore and he goes back to the port on the bus, actually three of them, to negotiate the shipping terms. Finally Massimo De Franceschi gives him the list of things to do and the price, two million Lire! Fortunately Lire have absolutely no value! They will accept only cash, but they will completely crate it and, hopefully send it on a ship to somewhere in the Port of Miami. They are very vague about when it will arrive in the U.S. and where it will really end up. It is amazing how trusting you can become, especially when dealing with Italians who can barely speak English. As we walk around town looking for more ATMs so we can gather together two million Lire, we are hoping that someone will steal the bike from in front of the hotel. Even though he doesn't lock it anymore no one takes it. Wrong hotel and wrong city! We are also sending some of our gear with the bike so we are down to a duffle bag each. Still too heavy, but we learn that later.

On our way back to the port to deliver the bike we make a wrong turn and suddenly we are on the autostrada going out of town. We have to take the toll ticket and then, finally, there is a place to make a U turn. Now we are heading back to that same toll booth. The man spends a lot of time trying to decide what to do with us and ostensibly writes down our license number, but we know he can't see it from inside the booth what with the huge pile of luggage hanging over the back of the bike and what will he do with it anyway. Then he lets us go. Beans also goes the wrong way on a one way street in front of three policemen. One waves us over and tries to talk to us, but we don't understand anything and he doesn't understand us so he finally shrugs and lets us go also. We are getting good at this.

We finally get the bike to Masini Transporti and count out two million Lire. Oops we are short by a few lire but he laughs and says it is ok. Beans goes through the same routine with the gas tank and the battery, then more paperwork, copies and lots of conversation in broken English. Bean're writes his name and address down on a blank sheet of paper and we walk away. He has nothing to prove that they have his bike or that they will ship it to the U.S.

Now we have to make all new plans and put together a different trip. Bean're would have liked to just repair it himself in the back of a shop, which he knows he can do, but the motor is still under a two year full warranty. It all goes against the sensibility of the totally self-reliant biker who can handle any situation at any time and he is really depressed. He suggests that maybe we should just go back to Munich and fly home early. I, of course, react with lots of tears and say I am not going home. If he wants to leave, I will rent a car and drive through Italy by myself. I am not ready to give up so soon. We decide we better get something to eat and try to get it all back to-gether. Over lunch we decide to try to continue the trip by train and ferry and will head for Morocco after all. So we buy train tickets to Barcelona, obviously we aren't thinking as straight as we think we are!

With time to kill before the train leaves, we shove our remaining luggage in a locker and Beans puts together a delightful and sponta-neous tour of the city of Genoa by bus! I do not know how he knew where we were going. He is a genius at knowing where he is. Our first stop is Ferrari Plaza which is absolutely gorgeous. A huge foun-tain with naked little children playing in the water, surrounded by stunning old buildings. He leads me down narrow, twisting and hilly alley-ways lined with little shops, shuttered for the long lunch hour. He buys us each a peach from a fruit stand, delicious, and our spirits are lifting. Then another large plaza down by the wharf where they are setting up a fair. Then in front of us is the Neptune, an old wood sailboat and we do the tourist thing, a tour and lots of pictures. Then on to the aquarium.

Now we are really tourists and have our picture taken next to a huge stuffed penguin!! This photo turns out to be fantastic. We are the greatest juxtaposition, which is what makes it all so wonderful! He is the quintessential biker with his long hair, red bandanna, wonderful tattoos and Italian "wife beater" T-shirt and I am all in black, sophisticated looking, if you don't know that I have been wearing this pair of black jeans for a week and probably slept in them at least once!. We both have relaxed and are having a great time. The aquarium goes on forever and ever with lots of surprises and it is quite wonderful. Penguins, dolphins, sharks, seals and even a Pesce Trombetta! A little trumpet fish in shocking red! Who knew?

Time to rush back to the train station and off we go to Ventiglia, Italy, on the border of France. We stop at every little town and some of them twice!! Not the upscale and speedy train we expected. There is no air conditioning, and even worse, there is no dining car! We speed along the Italian Riviera which consists of too many tacky buildings and rows of trailers that line the beautiful water front. There is a spectacular sunset after we change trains in France, but by the time we arrive in Marseilles we have had enough, no dining car and we don't want to spend the night trying to sleep sitting up. How did we forget to ask for first class? Oops, sorry I guess that should read, how did I forget? Anyway, we decide to leave the train. After a five-block walk - this is when we realize that we still have way too much luggage - we finally find a hotel with an available room. It is delightfully seedy. The Hotel Victory - where did they get that name? The faded and stained pink curtains are drooping, the bathroom is literally falling apart and the French doors open out to the street where they are celebrating something out there for most of the night, but we are very tired. Inspector Clouseau is not to be found!

In the morning we stop for delicious cafe au lait and breakfast at the boulangerie downstairs, before the forced march to the plaza and the subway ticket which translates to the bus ticket and the trip to the port looking for a ferry. Up and down stairs and over and around construction sites and we finally find a ferry office where they are lined up to go to Oran tomorrow. The only ferry today is to Algiers, our original destination when we had the bike. But now there isn't enough time to drive from Algiers to Casablanca. Time to reorganize again. Beans watches the luggage and I trek out to find some alternatives. It isn't easy. I finally find a large marine office where they oversee all the ferries. My French is not good and their English is as bad, but with the help of another passenger I finally find out that the only ferry to Tangiers doesn't leave until Tuesday, so that is the end of that idea. By the time I walk back I have decided that the only answer lies in taking a cab to the airport and then arranging for the next flight to Morocco. Expensive but who cares at this point and it is the only solution. There is nothing like a nice long taxi ride to soothe frazzled nerves. And Air France goes to Casablanca at 2:00 P.M., in just a few hours. Just enough time to eat two more meals.

And we are airborne again, to Morocco! We are actually going to get there. The flight is lovely and includes a full meal with great French rolls and brie. I get free red wine, two bottles. The second one I put in my suitcase for an emergency. Little did I know. Immigration and customs are pretty normal, and the first we have really seen since entering Europe in Munich. That will change too. The ladies bathroom has a man in it.... in a Muslim country?

Saturday night in Casablanca! We have made it and are very excited. First we have to rent a car. It is a very charming experience. We walk into the first car rental place, Thrifty, where there is a very young man behind the desk. He immediately gets excited and calls his boss and reports to us that he will be here right away, "10 minutes." Then he calls someone else who shows up immediately. Then someone else shows up to run for coffee for us, really good espresso. Then they alternate running to the money exchange place to find out the exchange rate for Dirhams. Everyone is very excited at the prospect of renting us a car. In between all this activity the young man entertains us with his imitation of shoot 'em up American cowboys. He and Beans are firing finger pistols back and forth across the desk with sound effects and much laughter. The boss arrives and after much negotiation and refiguring and discussion, we finally end up with a Fiat with no air conditioning. Beans doesn't like that and it is also too short, no room for his long legs. While they load the car and sign papers I discover a black and white cat and feed him my leftover brie, he's happy.

We are off in our little car that has no gas at all, looking for a gas station. They must siphon all the gas out when someone returns a car. Fortunately, we find a gas station immediately, I bet they do a great business. The attendants are very intrigued by the blond American with long hair and tattoos. He is surrounded by helpful Moroccans, laughing and trying to communicate. Then into Casablanca and Beans takes me on an incredible tour of the city: downtown, the port, the old city, miles and miles of the poor sections where everything is for sale on the street, from sides of meat hanging from the roof, to faucets and pipes and every possibility in between. They just set up on the sidewalk. And everyone is on the street also, walking or pushing a huge loaded cart or leading a donkey. It is all a little overwhelming. The noise, the smells, the poverty, the buildings, the exotic look of everything captures our imaginations.

The traffic is amazing. There are an incredible number of little cars on the roads, Fiats, Citroens, etc. all driving very fast and by their own set of rules . Add to that: donkey carts everywhere and huge push carts made with car wheels plus large horse drawn carts, and seriously overloaded flat bed trucks, with every possible thing piled high on top, double the height of the cab and sort of tied down, trying to maintain their balance and negotiate the traffic. It seems everyone has a scooter made from various spare parts wired together, and they are everywhere, darting through this incredible maze of vehicles. Every intersection becomes a traffic jam that looks hopeless as they turn left from any lane on a whim and seemingly obey red lights when they feel like it. For no discernible reason and without warning everyone will go right through a red light. And the pedestrians are everywhere and appear to think that it is perfectly safe to walk in the street. It is very intense. Somehow, once again Beans adjusts and goes with the flow. But he can't understand why they all drive way past the red light, into the intersection, where they can not possibly see the light change and then sit there until everyone in back blows their horn! This is repeated at every intersection by everyone who can possibly make it out that far. "Why can't they figure it out, makes no sense."

We finally settle on the Hotel Plaza. Small, nice and Moroccan. It has a funky old metal elevator that we can barely cram ourselves into, with double wood doors, and a very young bellhop who speaks no English but grabs our heavy duffle bags and runs up the stairs. Our room is wonderful with ten-foot high French doors opening out to a balcony facing a mosque, the medina and McDonalds, talk about juxtaposition.

We set everything down and off we go into a huge maze of sellers and hawkers unlike anything we could imagine. Everything is for sale from raw fish to leather jackets, herbs and vegetables to jewelry and shoes, bread and hubcaps, boiled snails and bicycles, hot nuts, wrought iron, lamps, clothes, fresh popcorn, copper tubing, barrettes and repaired scooters. We are harassed a little, and one man seemingly attempts to pick Beans pocket and tries to blame it on a little boy. There is a possibility of all this escalating, but Beans doesn't let it happen. It seems like we are completely lost, I am getting panicky, but Beans with his great sense of direction gets us out of this maze of humanity and shops, back to the main boulevard.

We've worked up an appetite and it is time for dinner. We pick a quiet little place with tables outside, across from the hotel and in front of the medina. The Restaurant Cannebiere, specialte poissons - fish - pescados. The host tries to explain the fish to us and we are only getting more confused. Thought he was describing Marlin but then he said, "no, a small fish." When in doubt, order the mixed seafood! Very leisurely they bring our cokes in bottles and then a wonderful assortment of Moroccan olives and bread. We are enjoying this immensely and then the seafood arrives. It is "sole" and mullet, very small and fried whole, a heap of small and very hot shrimp also cooked whole and sliced fried calamari. It looks beautiful and is delicious except for the "sole" which neither one of us likes. The woman-chef-half-owner, Haga, comes out from the kitchen to wish us bon appetite. We eat with our fingers and stuff ourselves again. Beans gets wonderful green tea served in a little clear glass with fresh mint and lights up a Cuban cigar that he bought in Genoa. We sit and enjoy it all. Haga is very proud of her "special" green tea.

We watch a white Citroen on the boulevard go past us and then he changes his mind and starts backing up a one way street, weaving through three lanes of oncoming traffic for more than a block, reaches the cross street and backs through, over to the other side of the boulevard where he continues to reverse the same block, but on the other side of the street, to where he wants to go. And this is done through traffic with speed but great calmness and nobody honks their horn.

Now Haga returns. She and Beans have a great conversation. She is very taken with him; shows him pictures of her children and grandchildren and gives him her card. The conversation continues and when we are finally ready to leave she asks us to sit with her and her husband. They are playing gin rummy. She tells Bean're that she is a medium and that he has a very big and good heart, but when he is angry, he is very angry. But he has a good balance. That he doesn't like to work and is an artist. She couldn't have made him happier. After learning our schedule, she insists that we come back on Tuesday night and she will make a very special couscous just for us. As we finally leave the restaurant at almost 11:00 P.M., she hugs us and blows kisses as we cross the street! She has insisted that he bring his card back right away. When he returns with it, he tells her when he visits Morocco again he will be riding his Harley Davidson and will park it right there in front of her restaurant and she says, next time you won't be staying at a hotel, you will stay at my house. It is all so very charming and delightful. A very intriguing place.

Watching Beans at the table tonight, leaning back, so thoroughly relaxed, enjoying his cigar and drinking in this exotic city along with his tea, I was trying to decide what it was about him that people were so quickly taken with him and why they liked him so much. I think one reason is because he is so exceptionally unique and always true to who he is, 100%. He doesn't try to adapt or change, he is himself always, and people recognize that and respect him for it and are fascinated by it. "That's cool."

We lie in bed, too excited to sleep and talk forever. Beans, "This isn't a trip of a lifetime, it is three trips of a lifetime." We wander out on the balcony to look at this incredible city. "You really had a good idea when you decided we should make this trip."

It is completely unpredictable, but without warning, the enormity of the differences, the strangeness, the smells, the poverty and the disturbingly exotic personality of this country, it completely overwhelms us.

It has also been another day of five meals: Breakfast in Marseilles. Two lunches at the airport. Third lunch on the plane. Dinner in Casablanca.

This morning Beans has made a decision; he is not driving this little Fiat across the desert with no room for his legs and without air conditioning. I try to convince him that it is going to be just like riding on the motorcycle, open the windows and enjoy the breeze and his response is a classic: "Don't piss on my leg and tell me it is raining!" Needless to say, we head back to the airport. It is a challenge to find, but there is always something to look at wherever we are. After much negotiation and discussion, veiled threats and hand wringing, we finally end up with a Mitsubishi 9 passenger mini bus, still without air conditioning, but with much more leg room and more of a presence on the road. Not exactly intimidating but better, and we look less like tourists unless, of course, they actually see us inside!! We do not blend in! Of course we didn't notice that one of the rear windows won't lock. Oh, well. Again they have rented us a car with absolutely no gas, so immediately we have to find that gas station and fill up. Once again Beans has a great rapport with the guys. We have four people pumping our gas and trying out their very limited English. They seem to be fascinated by Americans.

On our way out of town we are stopped by the police. There are roadblocks several times, but we are waved through. Then we are stopped, they wave a small little wand at you. We produce all our papers for the rental and his international drivers license and the policeman tries to communicate with us. He finally gives up and waves us on our way. Not speaking the language, either French or Arabic, is a big help.

As we drive the desert becomes devoid of any growth at all. There isn't a tumble weed blowing across the sand. The only green we see is just a very few shrubs by the wells that have been dug. It is desert like I have never seen before and it stretches forever, to the mountains way off in the distance. Every once in a while there will be a totally isolated adobe house and some signs of life. And out in the middle of absolutely nowhere will be a boy watching a flock of sheep. I cannot imagine what the sheep are eating. Camels stride along hauling bundles, along with a lot of donkeys loaded down with huge containers of water and/or people. It is an incredible scene and we cannot comprehend what their lives are like out here in this sand. The strangeness again is overwhelming.

The road just continues on like a shimmering mirage, in a straight line in front of us, across this flat expanse of sand toward the mountains, way off in the distance.

Suddenly, in the middle of nowhere there is a restaurant, all by itself. Naturally, we are starving so... There is a small boy and a man in the yard in front and they hurry inside behind the counter way in the back to serve us. How strange we must look. They speak no English and we are getting nowhere. No matter what we say he continues to point to the eggs sitting in a bowl on the counter, so Beans switches to French and orders two omelets with fromage. A young girl has appeared and the man immediately gives her the order and sends her to the prepare "au cuisine." The food is good and the bread, large flat rounds cooked on an open fire, is wonderful. We are soon stuffed again. The WC is the expected hole in the ground and a bit scary, but usable. The kids, of course, are adorable.

As we drive along, suddenly we are alongside train tracks. It is the Marrakech Express!

This city is amazing. Very pretty and colorful. We have eaten McDonalds on three continents now! Fortified with cheeseburgers and fries, Beans quickly finds the main medina and then a small hotel on the comer. Hotel Taz is charming and very Moroccan and next to all the activity. While checking into the hotel he meets a guide, Asjih, who will take us shopping after we have cleaned up. His suggestion. We must look really bad. They even have parking in a huge garage. A quick shower and we are off to the medina with our guide. The government now licenses the guides and they have to wear an ID card. No one else is allowed to take you anywhere or show you anything. We want to avoid the insanity of our experience trying to shop in Casablanca and this seems to be the answer. There are 1,600,000 people in Marrakech and over 25,000 shops in this one medina!

I have warned Beans about the rug sellers and their green tea, so the first place our guide takes us is to his rug salesman. "We are not buying a rug." "Oh, no just to look. Show you historic house with beautiful rugs. Not to buy just to look." And we are off through winding walkways behind buildings to the antique house and up-stairs. "Would you like some tea?" Ah, it has all begun and we knew better, but here we are. Lots of tea and lots of rugs spread out in front of us. "Just to look, not to buy" ... He keeps directing the boys to bring more rugs to spread out at our feet. Very beautiful, but we can't afford to buy a rug. "Just feel how wonderful they are". And we are in the middle of the room feeling the rugs. "But we can't buy a rug." "If you were going to buy one which one do you like the best... this one?" How are we ever going to get out of here? Finally they realize that we are really not going to buy a rug at any price and give up.

The guide leads us back into the medina and more adventure. He does show us a nice silver place and I buy a few pieces and he gives us gifts of silver pieces hanging on silk thread, very pretty. Then to the leather man to find snakeskin belts. The Moroccans don't like to sell snakes so they hide the skins. We meet Mustafah, the leather man. His head is shaved and he is very charming and funny and sends a little boy off to bring back the belts. The booth is filled with camel skin made into everything you can possibly imagine and he is busy trying to sell Beans something. The boy comes running back with the belts and we each pick out one. Then Beans mentions that he is looking for saddle bags for the Knucklehead. Now Mustafah's eyes light up. Oh, he has Harley Davidson saddle bags. The little boy is sent off again. I wonder how far he has to run for this stuff. Meanwhile, they are negotiating the price of the belts.

Beans has found his forte and he is bargaining hard. Mustafah: "You bargain like Berber." There are more serious negotiations when the camel skin saddle bags arrive. They really are very nice with little pockets on top of the bags. I am no help and seem to be working on the wrong side! Mustafah tells Beans he will give him 5,000 camels for me! What a great guy! Beans immediately shakes hands on that deal! How much is a camel worth?

THE JOURNEY CONTINUES ON PAGE 177

DOWN UNDER

163

BEAN'RE IN EUROPE

16. **BIKER PART**
MALCHOW

NINE PART TWO

TOUR OF EUROPE AND MOROCCO
BY NERISSE TROMBETTA

THE JOURNEY CONTINUED
FROM PAGE 160

"How do you say full of shit in Arabic?" "No plastic fantastic." "You are Ali-Baba" "My father make bags by hand!" "Almost free." "Just like free." All this is bargaining language. I am laughing so hard. They finally agree on a price and then start over because Beans decides he wants the bags separated at the top. Now there is an added discussion about how soon they can have this ready because we are leaving tomorrow morning. I am making comments about his poor father having to stay up all night to make a new set of saddlebags by hand in the dark ... Mustafah is laughing with us and enjoying the jokes and bargaining as much as we are. They finally agree on the price and the delivery time of 9:00 A.M. at the hotel. Meanwhile, I have found a great orange fringed purse to throw into the bargain.

We are off again with the guide who is taking us to his friends who try to sell us everything. We buy sodas out on the plaza, take pictures with the men who sell water in wild red clothes and fringed hats. They carry goat skins filled with water and little metal cups around their necks. We will stick with the bottled water, thank you. Beans has his picture taken with a cobra and rattlesnake.

It is time to find the ATM again. The machines are everywhere, but here the trick is to find one that is working. It is amazing how in every country now you can put your card in, push some buttons and out comes the correct currency, usually more than we need. Then we stroll back to the hotel for dinner, which is a wonderful buffet of Moroccan food. The lamb stew is delicious. There are wonderful salads and fruit, but we are leery and skip them. We are entranced by this city and the charming people. There are no beggars, but everyone is selling something. As we sit at the dinner table by the window little children come by selling jewelry and small packages of Kleenex. They offer it through the open window quietly, hiding in the shadows, so the waiters will not notice and chase them away. I am buying everything from them, of course.

We sit outside on the front steps of the hotel and watch the scene, with a cigar. The waiter comes out to joke with Beans and he goes upstairs to get a cigar for him, too. He is very pleased.

The scene on the street is amazing. It is late and the Moroccans are now out walking. Families with little children eating green ice cream cones. Women in full veils strolling together and younger women in western dress. The streets are full. After we have watched too many people go by with those ice cream cones, we decide to go look for them. Just down the street there is a little machine on the street. It is pistachio! It is delicious and it is two dirhams.

The next morning at breakfast, Mustafah shows up exactly at 9:00 A.M. with the saddlebags! We are surprised. He charges them on Visa everyone here has credit card machines. We are having such a great time in Marrakech that we have decided to stay for part of the day and skip Fes and Meknes which would be a very long drive. Mustafah suggests that he could take us around even though he isn't allowed to do that. He can get a special card that he is our friend and therefore can go with us. So we arrange to meet him at his shop in an hour. "It is very easy to find, just go straight in and keep going" Oh, sure. Our guide from yesterday sees us and starts giving Beans the hard sell for seeing the palace and other sights with him. I am backing away from this discussion and suddenly see a man behind Asjih who is making a very strange motion ... he touches the guide's behind with his palm and then kisses his fingers and returns his hand to his bottom. It is the sign for ass kisser! I can add that to my collection.

We escape Asjih and head for the medina by ourselves with our directions. We are wandering around forever. We pass a really wonderful silver shop where, surprisingly there is no pressure to buy and I find a fabulous ring and bracelets for gifts. Beans sees a beautiful white, hand embroidered cotton caftan and immediately knows that it is the perfect gift for Sunny, a friend in Miami.

Back out into the maddening crowd of the medina where everyone wants to sell you everything, to try and find Mustafah. We keep passing that rug salesman and are about to give up when the little boy shows up out of nowhere. He has been sent to find us and tells us to follow him. He takes off at a run until he is about 30 feet ahead of us, so we can just catch glimpses of him in the crowd. He can't be seen leading us anywhere! Every once in awhile when we think we have lost him he pops up, standing on something high and grins. Finally, there is the leather booth and Mustafah. There is much laughter. "Do you want some green tea?" Yes, we do. It is so good and again the glasses are filled with mint leaves. Now we are friends talking and laughing sitting on little stools near the floor. Mustafah wants Beans to teach him some pick up lines for the American girls. This is a challenge. He suggests "You look like Marilyn Monroe," only for the blond girls. And "Bootylicious." Mustafah is writing these down phonetically in Arabic in his little book! He has no idea what they mean and we try to explain. He laughs hard at bootylicious. So now I want to know how to sign F you. It is just like the Italian so that is not new.

Beans wants to buy T-shirts so Mustafah gets the little boy to surreptitiously take us to the right booth. They have embroidered T-shirts and we buy several. Then they are selling us Moroccan hand embroidered shirts. Our gifts are turbans and/or veils. They wrap them around our heads for pictures. Beans trying to blend in again. Especially here, he is such a contrast with his blue eyes, long blond hair and tattoos. The children and teenagers here are so fascinated. One or two are bold and try to touch his tattoos. I am sure that he is changing the style in this country. The boys will all be growing their hair and looking for a tattoo parlor.

Back to Mustafah's and we trade e-mail addresses. He wants us to stay tonight so we can go to the disco with him. But we have decided to travel again. We walk back to the hotel through the plaza. At least we can find our way home.

It is time for lunch and we enjoy our hotel and waiter so much that we decide to eat there again. He is delighted to see us and we order from the menu. Beans is getting a terrine of beef, recommended by the waiter. It arrives with quite a bit of fanfare, in the typical Moroccan pottery with the tent shaped cover. The waiter sets it down carefully and elaborately warns him not to touch the dish as it is very hot! So Beans has to touch it and announces to me that it is cold ... There is some discussion and then the waiter, with ceremony, lifts the top off and the plate is completely empty. Now he is really enjoying his own joke. After much laughter he brings the correct dish.

Moroccans have surprised us with their very positive attitudes, always and their incredible sense of humor. They love a good joke and love to laugh and poke fun.

While checking his e-mail down the street, Beans learns that Jimi Hendrix and Janis Joplin had houses in Essaouira, always pronounced Sa-wear-a, but spelled differently on every map and every sign. We even saw Esaquira, a little town on the coast and the ride is supposed to be great, so we check out of the hotel and head west.

SEPTEMBER 10, 2001

Back into the desert. Once we are in the mountains every turn promises to open up to the ocean. Finally there it is and Essaouira is there, too. As we descend we come upon two men and their camel along the side of the road. Must stop here and take pictures. They are selling rides on Namoon and soon we are both astride and the camel laboriously rises. They lead us around until the pictures will include Essaouira in the background. The ride is much more comfortable than I expected. Getting back down is more

disconcerting. "One hundred dirham for the camel and 50 for me"
They laugh at their joke. Lots of fun.

This idyllic town sits right on the water and after all the desert,
looks lush, tropical and wonderful. The very wide beach stretches
the length of the town and then there is a large harbor filled with
fishing boats and a small boat building operation where they are
building very large boats. There are four unfinished and the heavy
ribs of the unfinished boats are exposed and thrusting up towards
the sky.

It seems that everyone is on the beach along with men and
camels selling more rides. We find a hotel facing the beach, Hotel
Iles, La passion de I'Hotellerie de Qualite . Very nice, a large room
with French doors opening to the ocean view.

Dinner is at Bab Laachour, a restaurant down the street, on
the second floor, with tables on an open air balcony facing the harbor and plaza. Delicious fish soup, more wonderful olives and
bread, sausage and pommes frites, terrine de veau and coffee for
80 dirham, about four dollars. The plaza below us is fascinating.
As the evening progresses more and more women appear in bright
colored veils. Their children quietly play while their sedate moth-
ers stroll across the plaza talking together. In front of the bright
lights on the wall surrounding the plaza, the children play huge
shadow games, creating monsters with their bodies.

After a cigar we stroll also, towards the wharf, past more
restaurants where they display their fresh fish. You can pick out
what you want and they cook it for you. A veiled woman sits with
her calico cat curled in her lap. It is a complex and they are making
phosphate! The size of the pipe overflowing into the ocean is
frightening. I am trying to take pictures as we speed along ...
Beans starts calling me Erin Brockovich. This town has obviously
grown as workers were drawn to the jobs here. I wonder what
their lives are like, not to mention their health.

We are hungry again and there is nothing to choose from, then suddenly we see a large open air restaurant. Looks good to us. A little boy has designated himself as the car-watcher and makes sure we have locked everything up. There is a row of very competitive fish sellers with their seafood displayed on ice in front of their stoves. We make our choices, after we get free tastes and sit down at a nice table. There is a lot of laughter and banter back and forth among the sellers and their helpers. Soon we have cokes and then the seafood starts to arrive. Mountains of whole fried shrimp, fried calamari, and whole small fish along with a loaf of French bread for each of us. We stuff ourselves. There is a slight disagreement about price and then we are back on the road, feeling better, but not for long.

I decide to skip the bathroom experience here and opt for a stop on the side of the road. He has to stop somewhere, sometime. And sure enough suddenly we round a bend and there in front of us is an incredible view that goes down and on forever with the beautiful ocean in the background. While he is setting up the shot, I am creating a puddle in the sand. Desperation!

Back on the road in our funky mini bus. Suddenly the American rock and roll stops and everyone is speaking in French or Arabic on every station, and we have no idea what is going on. Beans picks out the English words: World Trade Center, terrorists, Air Force One, Boston and Washington DC. We begin to speculate but can't imagine. He finally hears part of an English sentence as it is being translated into French and now we know two planes hit the World Trade Center. We are very concerned and frustrated at not knowing what is going on, but can not possibly imagine the enormity. Beans says maybe it is World War Ill.

It is hours before we reach Casablanca and we know so little that we can't even hypothesize what could have happened. The people in the hotel don't speak English and there are no TVs, so Bean're goes across the street to ask Haga. She tells him that the Japanese flew two planes into the World Trade Center. When he comes to the room to report this piece of puzzling news, we are really confused and beginning to get scared and paranoid. There are no English papers reporting this yet so he heads off for the internet office to get some information, after changing T shirts. It no longer seems smart to wear one printed with a large American Flag.

I wait for him to return in the slowly darkening room. There is that bottle of red wine from Air France. I dig it out and sit by the window looking out at the mosque across the street and watching for him to return. After awhile I start to get paranoid, what if he doesn't come back. But then I am reassured by the thought of Haga and her husband, who I know will help me no matter what happens and do what ever they have to do to find him.

He finally returns with a small sheaf of papers which he quietly and carefully sets down on the table. "I don't know if you want to read this." I am shocked by his demeanor and expression which scares me more and I leave the papers on the table. We lie down and he lights a cigar which we share in the dark room, as he relates some of the news to me. We can not comprehend it, naturally, and it is all compounded by being in a Muslim country. We are lying there listening to the Muslim call to evening prayer. It is surreal and we feel mentally and physically ill. And we are faced with decisions about our own safety.

We finally decide that we have to eat and we must show up for Haga's dinner. We sit way in the back of the restaurant where we can't be seen from the street. The couscous, loaded with lamb and squash, is delicious, but we can barely swallow a bite. The owner comes to talk to us, but we can't even do that at this point, especially since he still thinks it is the Japanese. We later realize that when Donald Rumsfeld said, "It is a second Pearl Harbor." they took this literally, which is how they would understand it. Finally we make our deepest apologies to him and excuse ourselves.

Back at the hotel we are feeling sicker and now realize that what we ate for lunch is making us ill. The front desk calls us, I didn't even know we had a phone. There is someone to see us. Bean're goes down and returns with a gallon of vanilla ice cream and gifts, a beautiful blue bowl and ash tray decorated with brass, from Haga and her husband. Their kindness makes us feel so much better. And the ice cream is wonderful. How did they know that it would be the only thing we could possibly eat. In the dark in our hotel room in downtown Casablanca, we share ice cream out of the huge container, eating with the tiniest plastic spoons. It is a little piece of familiarity and comfort in this totally strange and exotic country, when we really need it.

Haga has sent a message that she wants to talk to me so I reluctantly dress and go over to her restaurant. She is on her cell phone frantically trying to reach her son in New York City. Apparently she has been calling all afternoon and only getting a busy signal. I explain that her son is not living close to the World Trade Center and is probably fine and that it will be days or weeks before she can call him on the phone, as everything has been destroyed. Plus everyone is trying to call New York at the same time. She feels a little better and we try to comfort each other with hugs. The irony is that her son Miko, a Muslim, is in the US studying to be a pilot. The circle is so small in this big world. We talk for a while more and when I get ready to leave she insists on giving me more gifts. Their concern and graciousness has helped two bereft Americans more than they can know.

It is a very long night for many reasons. We have decided that although we have plane reservations for 5:00 P.M. tomorrow, we want to leave Morocco as soon as possible. We are unable to reach the airlines by phone or the American Embassy in Marrakech. We don't know enough to know what to expect. How nervous should we be? Will the airport be jammed with people trying to leave tomorrow? Are we in any danger here?

We don't even know what to be concerned about. We had been so in love with Morocco and the people and now we only want to get out as fast as we can. There is nothing familiar here to comfort us; not the food, the language, the customs, or the sounds, not even the bed or the pillows. All the things that we had loved now are making us extremely uncomfortable. And we yearn for home or something at least more familiar.

And to make us completely miserable, we are now physically very ill from lunch. The Moroccan crud has finally caught up with us. We spend the night alternating turns in the bathroom. The next morning Beans is still attempting to be humorous and shares more than I want to know, but by he middle of the day, he is too sick to even tease me. Our stomachs hurt like someone has been kicking us from the inside all night.

We have gone to the airport early and he sleeps on a bench. We try to find something that we hope our stomachs will digest. The choice is very limited. I opt for a fromage sandwich with lots of French bread and I give most of the cheese to a yellow and white cat inside the terminal. There are very few people in the airport. The opposite of what we expected. We didn't realize how afraid everyone would be to fly. We have a long quiet wait, but have lost the excitement of being in Morocco and only want to sit here and wait for the plane. The English paper finally arrives late in the afternoon and we devour it, trying to understand.

It is Bean're's turn for a bathroom experience, In the men's room at the airport there is a woman attendant. Not too unusual if you are somewhere other than in a Muslim country. As he opens the stall door she pushes him aside and goes in, wipes the seat and flushes the toilet and then indicates that he can enter. Now that is service!

Finally we can board the plane and leave for Marseilles. A quiet subdued flight, we arrive at 10:00 P.M. And seeing the long line of people waiting for a taxi without a taxi in sight, we take off walking again. Will we ever learn? We expect three blocks, but of course every hotel is full and we are walking forever. I finally tell him I can't go any further and sit down on my luggage at the curb. He takes off by himself and finds a room down a narrow alley. The lobby is on the second floor ... can we make it? Men are sitting around a table in their undershirts playing cards and give us the once over, as we drag ourselves up another flight to the room. And I am being generous calling it that. This is the worst. The bed sinks in the middle so badly you have to hold onto the edge. There is only a very gray top sheet that I am not interested in touching. There are no towels, no toilet paper or soap. The paint is peeling in great chunks off the walls and the linoleum is disgustingly dirty and undulates. But the room does have big French doors with beautiful ornate brass latches under 30 coats of paint. I may be sick but I can still see that. I tell the Beans to work on removing the latches during the night so we can have them as souvenirs, but he ignores me, as usual. The room does have one redeeming feature - it is the only available room in this part of Marseilles.

Then it gets cold. The temperature plunges. And of course the doors are warped and don't close. First I put on a second long sleeve shirt, then get up and add socks and finally put on my jeans over pajama bottoms. And wish I still had my gloves! The cold did not slow down the mosquitos, we are both badly bitten. "Are you sure those were mosquitos?" Some things are better off remaining unknown.

When we wake up the next morning, we are not in the best of moods and can hardly drag ourselves out of bed. Then discover that we have slept too late and missed our 9:30 train to Paris (neither one of us had a watch at any time during this trip). Hurrying is a waste of time, but we rush out to the street and find a taxi and miss our train. After much confusion we find another train leaving shortly and make sure we are in first class! Grab a petite dejeuner, sodas and all the English newspapers we can find. Suddenly there is security. The army is there checking passports and train tickets before we are allowed to walk to the train.

First class is so much better, isn't that a surprise? They actually serve food in a little stand-up sandwich bar. And we are going through beautiful Provence on our way to Paris. The scenery is beautiful and we chat with a couple from Guadalajara, he is French and she is French and Mexican. Very nice and their English is excellent. It is comforting to talk to them, although none of us mention the horror of the World Trade Center.

In Paris we grapple with the luggage again, we are back to hauling three duffle bags and it is not fun. A taxi to Gare L'Oest and we find lockers and get rid of it. They are scanning us and the luggage in and out of the baggage locker room. The military is armed with automatic assault weapons at ready, patrolling the station. They all look like they are 17 years old.

We try to call Lufthansa or Lauda Air to find out if they are flying yet and get nowhere. We have three hours to wait for the next train to Munich and Beans chooses to visit the Eiffel Tower. It is a great choice as we go all the way to the top and can see all of Paris. It is a beautiful day. Security is very visible here also. We buy key rings, very uncomfortable in your pocket, and more postcards, a good sign of recovery. Of course, we had to eat and choose hot dogs stuffed down the center of a loaf of French bread, while we enjoy the view. Then walk all the way down from level two. We run the last half as we suddenly realize that we could easily miss our train, again. I am rooting for missing it and staying in Paris, but the taxi driver makes it in time. I love this city and would love to spend the night. The security at the train station is even more visible and our tickets and identification are checked again before we board the train.

At Strasbourg, on the border we have to leave the car at the end of the train and run all the way with our three duffle bags, to the front half of the train, which is the only part that will continue to Munich. Then we walk and bump our way through six more cars to find an empty compartment where we can close the curtains and stretch out.

Once we stow the duffle bags, Beans heads out to the bathroom and two large German men are in his way. He tries to go around them as the car lurches and they block him. Suddenly he is backing into the compartment with the two Germans. A typical communication problem, finally, in English, "Passport, please." It is security without uniforms.

The dining car is the best and we take advantage of it. The food is delicious and the service great, just what we need. Then we sack out, stretched out over six wonderful seats. Sometime in the middle of the night I wake up to discover we are stopped at Augsburg, and realize that we aren't far from our stop. My fool proof plan is to sit up and therefore, not fall back asleep. Well, at least I wake up again at our stop, Passing, and in a mad rush we exit the train at 3:00 A.M. with almost all our belongings. Now to figure out the subway system, again. We go down the stairs and up the wrong stairs and have to do it all again to catch the last subway to Hauptbahnof station.

Soon we have reached downtown Munich and are checking into the Eden Hotel Wolff. Quite a change from the night before. This is a five-star hotel and really wonderful. Dragging our luggage down the halls at this hour is awful. I guess the bellhop is sleeping. Beans collapses on the floor in a dead end hallway with a heap of duffle bags and laughter. Eventually we go down the right hall and find the room. We are both feeling awful, but are soothed by wonderful beds with thick, fluffy down comforters and all the luxury to comfort us. The bathroom is really great, all pink marble. And there is TV. It has been over two days since we found out about the tragedy in New York and this is the first television we have seen. We lie in bed and watch CNN, BBC and MSNBC and try to comprehend the enormity of what has happened to our country and the world. We also watch some German news reports which show 200,000 people in Berlin at Brandenberg gate singing Amazing Grace and other local candle vigils and gatherings in honor of the many dead Americans.

BEANS DISCOVERS ROOM SERVICE

We indulge again. In the morning, our tongues have turned black! It looks like an inch thick of black fuzz coating. This cannot be a good sign. Our food poisoning is working its way out of every orifice.

We go out to the airport to personally check for the earliest flight, but no one is flying yet. We do get a reservation for Tuesday morning. It is time to regroup one more time. We can't just stay in a hotel and watch CNN for four days. Time to get out the map. There are four large cities within about a six to eight hour train ride: Salzburg, Paris, Florence and Amsterdam. Surprisingly, Florence is the closest, but we aren't going there. One more day of luxuriating in our 5 star hotel and a spectacular free breakfast and we pack for our trip to Amsterdam. I spend 20 minutes laboriously cutting my luggage in half, painstakingly deciding which clothes I won't need in Amsterdam and putting them into a garbage bag. (I always wanted to check out of a 5 star hotel with garbage bag luggage.) When I have finally finished, Beans picks up his sweatshirt, shorts and shave kit off the floor and throws it into my duffle bag, "There I'm packed."

The train station is right across the street and we stuff the unneeded luggage in a locker. A train for Amsterdam is leaving in 20 minutes. This system is fantastic. The train is beautiful and very streamlined in white and red. This is the train he had expected in the beginning and Beans wants photos in front of it. We are more experienced train riders now and stock up on oranges, bananas, fries, water, sprite, magazines and newspapers. We are ready. Inside we find an empty compartment, very plush, first class. Another couple joins us and then abruptly leaves. Was it Beans' fart? Whatever, at least we are by ourselves.

We are back to laughter and fun, not 100%, but much better. We make paper airplanes and sail them in the compartment. Someone told Beans he would never be able to travel with a woman for three weeks, said we wouldn't make it. He was wrong. We are into an unexpected fourth week and getting along great! There have been ups and downs, of course, but we have never argued or lost our temper. When things didn't go perfectly one of us would help the other out of their mood. And we have virtually been together the whole time. Except when Beans checked his email and went snow boarding by himself, and of course the times he snuck out in the middle of the night! He is even posing for photos, even undid his hair and brushed it out. You're so vain!. Tossing and fluffing and posing with it, pulled across his mouth. This is fun, traveling with the Beans.

The train ride is wonderful. From Mannheim to Amsterdam we have a dining car. We sit down at a little table with white linen and a wonderful waiter, just like the movies. We start with magnificent potato soup, then goulash for me and pasta for him. And cassis and creme for dessert. All the while watching beautiful scenery. We take pictures from the train window. The Rheine (Rhine) river, moving very rapidly with huge loaded barges, ferries and tour boats, for some reason, only going up stream. Castles on top of every hill and mountain and very picturesque little towns.

We arrive in Amsterdam at night and it is very intimidating for me. People everywhere. It is very crowded, few cars, lots of bicycles and cobblestone streets, broad tiled sidewalks and store after store. I am feeling way out of my element, tagging around after Beans as we look for a hotel room. It is a pretty city with beautiful buildings, but dirty. People throw their garbage everywhere on the street and in the trains. The little street cleaning machines go by with little effect. They are rolling joints everywhere, you can get high walking past an open doorway. Beans is anxious to get off by himself, but we can't find a room. After checking with the tourist offices it is apparent that The Grand has the only vacancy in the whole city and it is an apartment for $450. US. We are exhausted from walking and looking but not that tired. We are told that the closest vacancy will be in Utrecht, 20 minutes away by train. Back to the station.

Beans, we are not in Germany, anymore! On the train a black man is smoking a joint and drinking beer and he did not buy a train ticket. "The man" is going to write him up for not buying a train ticket, everything else is legal. He counters with, "But I already have a ticket for this," which he shows the conductor, and then, "the trains never run on time and the service is bad, I shouldn't have to buy a ticket." Great logic especially for someone who obviously never pays.

We finally check into the Holiday Inn! Much better than it sounds and only $110. A large, very nice room; and room service. A nice restaurant and great little bar at the top of the hotel, with a great view. Beans gets dinner in bed and we watch Pulp Fiction.

The next morning after a great breakfast and beautiful view from the top of the hotel, I am ready to shop. I can not wear these jeans another day and do not want to think about how long it has been. We split up and I am into the department store, buying weird black pants and a white cotton shirt, then I walk the city for hours, dodging the rain which sometimes comes down in torrents, but only for moments. I find Rick's Cafe, and idyllic canals with pristine little motor boats, coffee in a small smoke filled shop, and then off to USA Pizza to meet him. The streets are very crowded, even in the rain. We walk together down the tiny streets and smaller alleys and find the red light district with girls in skimpy underwear standing and posing behind full length glass doors. The alleyway is very narrow and the girls are very close. A red light bar is above the doors. It is surreal, each like a live picture from Playboy. And they all look super perfect to me. Beans says he doesn't see anything he likes, or words to that effect, just to be politically correct.

We find a little Italian place for lunch, totally empty and therefore pot-smoke free. Hard to find a restaurant where we won't be getting high on second-hand smoke. Spliffs hang in the store windows, only seven gilders, about $3.50 each. An entirely different atmosphere and level of frivolity than we have seen anywhere else.

Later, at our hotel, we go up to the Railroad Bar on the 22nd floor. It overlooks the huge railroad and subway stations below. There is constant activity, trains coming and going. It is hypnotizing. I indulge in brandy alexanders and we have dinner in bed again - that good room service!

Back to Munich on the train, which means another great meal in the dining car. We share a table with a girl and her dog, a wonderful and relatively large black and white mutt, under the table. Beans slips food to him.

We get to the airport three hours early on Tuesday and there are security checks after security checks. They search our luggage before checking it through. They check our passports over and over and hand search everything we are carrying on board and then pat us down. Once we are in the secure section, they announce that our flight has been delayed because of mechanical problems in Vienna and there will be an additional four-hour wait. We read, we eat, we sleep and we talk to the other passengers who are waiting. Some were on this same flight last Tuesday when the plane was sent all the way back to Munich. The pilot was honest about what had happened, but after over 10 hours in the air they were back where they started, in Munich. There is a surprising amount of humor among these people. No one is complaining. Every 15 minutes a voice on the loud speaker announces that no one will be allowed to take knives or scissors in their carry on luggage. We board our flight, finally and shortly after take off they serve us dinner. Each and every one of us is given a stainless steel knife!

Thank you for the movies to distract us and make the time pass. We finally arrive in Miami, clear immigration and almost make it through customs, except for that orange leftover from Munich. And almost a month later, after emails and many phone calls, Beans suddenly gets an email from Genoa that his motorcycle is in Miami, safe and sound. You can trust those Italians.

TEN PART 1

AUSTRALIAN TOUR

One Adventure just kind of blends into the next.

Bean're goes global once again – Bean're's journal of the trip to and through Australia.

As many of you already know I will be leaving for Australia on Nov 3rd. I will be there for two months. I wanted to go to Asia also, but time, funds and political uprisings are prohibiting me from doing that leg of the journey. No worries though I'm sure two months will just be the tip of the iceberg in getting to know the real Australia.

Getting ready for this trip was a little stressful even for me. Instead of shipping my bike from Miami it was cheaper to start from LA, so what would you do? I did the same, jumped on my bike and rode out. It just so happened that my friends at The Horse magazine were throwing their first annual West Coast Smokeout/Chopper Show in Cottonwood, AZ. Perfect. I had a great time there and can't wait to go back next year. After that was over I rode out west and visited my good friend East LA Georgie. I was able to stay at his house while I crated the bike and hauled it to the airport shipper. My bike doesn't like long boat rides so it was flown over. Besides, I can't live without my bike for that long, two weeks is long enough.

I've flown back to Miami and I'm waiting for my flight to Australia. This weekend is Fantasy Fest in Key West. I guess as long as I am waiting I might as well go down there and kill some time.

OFF TO A ROARING START

My trip is 21 hours long. Sounds kind of long huh? Well it just got longer. I had a one-hour layover in San Francisco. The plane was two hours late taking off from Miami so I knew I would miss my connecting flight. I flew American Airlines across America. A two-thousand dollar ticket and they still charged me four dollars for a box of pretzels and snacks. Since they did cause me to miss my flight on Quantas, they put me up in a swanky hotel here in San Francisco for two days until I can catch the next flight to Melbourne.

This brings me to another scare. I shipped my bike with DHL. I flew my crated bike from LA to Melbourne, Australia two weeks ago. My cell phone (which was my contact number) has a Melbourne, Florida area code. When my bike arrived in Melbourne last week they saw that I was in Melbourne, FL and called thinking that they made a mistake and would send the bike to me in Fl. No, I assured them, and I'm hoping they hold it for a couple more days now as I really don't need anymore surprises.

I guess I'm off to get a rental car and kill some more time. Until tomorrow when I can catch my plane and continue my journey, I will make the best of this.

THE EAGLE HAS LANDED

I have finally arrived in Melbourne. My 18-hour non-stop flight from San Francisco included a-two hour layover and a change of planes in Sidney. They assured me it was non-stop with only fuel stops. I am finally here so I won't dwell on the details. My mind is almost shot anyways from jet lag. I feel like I am having flashbacks from my Grateful Dead days. That combined with the differences of this country, it's like being in an episode of Twilight Zone. I also lost one whole day due to crossing the international time zone. That really puts into perspective just how far away Australia is. I didn't just leave my time zone, I left a whole days' worth of time zones not to mention I am also on the other side of the equator which means it is coming on summer here.

Time to get some sleep and pick the bike up in the morning. Today is a holiday due to the Australian Derby (horse race). Tomorrow I will be well rested and pick up my bike and start this trip.

ANOTHER OBSTACLE

When I hit adversity I feel that it I am on the right track. The way I see it the good things aren't easy, but if we strive we can make them happen. This trip is going to be a remarkable experience, but its not just going to make itself happen. I thought I had everything in order, but yesterday I found that my bike, which I was told last week was ready to pick up, isn't ready at all. It seems that customs is holding it 'till I get a broker to do the paper work and get the inspections done. It may even have to be quarantined. So I am stuck here waiting in limbo and forced to ride public transportation in Melbourne until I can get my bike.

This is just more proof to me that this will be an awesome trip, when it does finally begin.

MORE PROBLEMS

I am having a lot of trouble clearing customs, there's a new problem which must be resolved before I can go any farther. In Australia they have VICROADS which is the equivalent of the DMV. They have to do an inspection, to make sure that the vehicle is safe. My 10 over front end and no turn signals are a definite red flag. I may be able to waive that though since I am a temporary tourist who will be taking the bike home with me when I go. There is no waiving of the import tax of 1800 dollars though. It may or may not be refundable. Seems there are things like this that are unclear and no one knows for sure. I also need to get insurance, but first I need an Australian drivers license and registration. I believe I have found someone to help with these last two items.

Someone here who has helped me tremendously is a man named David Reidie. He owns Harley City (770 Sydney Road Brunswick, Victoria, AU 3056). He is a well known biker here. He owns many vintage Harleys, all of them are in the museum at his shop. He also races them in the vintage races they have here for pre-1957 motorcycles. I have posted pictures on my web site www.beanre.com, of David standing by Burt Munro's real 1920 Indian, the basis for the Worlds Fastest Indian movie. It seems that David is from New Zealand and lived a couple blocks from Burt.

A DAY AT THE RACES!

My latest day was spent at the race track. This week it's been the Melbourne Cup Race week. Horses from all over the world come here to race. The crowd is over 100,000 everyday. Being from Kentucky and having attended many races, including several Kentucky Derbys, I had to make an appearance. I picked the Oaks Day, which also happened to be ladies day. It was very formal so if I hadn't been wearing my rings, the Baker wife beater T shirt may not have been formal enough. Everyone was super friendly and eager to speak to this Yank. My favorite wager is an exacta ticket, which they did not have here. As they say, "no worries," I couldn't pick a winner all day much less the first and the second.

A lot of people ask me about the water swirling backwards in the drains over here. That is true as well as the cars and the trains running on the opposite side of the road. I wasn't prepared for the horses running clockwise around the track. That's opposite of what they do in the states. Maybe that's why I couldn't pick a winner. "no worries," even the losers get lucky sometime.

Meanwhile I am back to riding public transportation until my bike is released.

VENTURING OUTSIDE OF THE CITY

I woke up early to get out of the city and into the Yarra Valley which is in the foothills of the Blue Mountains (the eucalyptus trees release chemicals which tend to scatter the sunlight which in turn gives the area a bluish tint when viewed from a distance). At Yarra valley I rode an antique steam locomotive up into the hills and ended up at the Fergusson Winery in the heart of the wine growing area. There were many wineries all around and everyone was giving away plenty of free samples, but I couldn't find any non-alcoholic versions (something I have yet to find in Australia) so I stuck to water. Fergusson's also has a restaurant with a fire pit big enough to roast a whole roast of beef. The Australian beef is incredible. There is such a difference that I can even taste a difference in a McDonalds hamburger.

My next stop was at the Healesville Sanctuary. It's an animal reserve with native animals including several endangered species. I was there for several hours. While I was there I noticed some swelling in my elbow and a tender spot. As the day progressed the swelling grew and grew. I did not see a bite mark, but thought that's what it was. When I returned to the city at around 5:30 P.M. my elbow and lower arm were really swollen and the elbow was getting hard to bend.

In Australia they sell a lot of prescription drugs over the counter so I went to a drugstore (they call them chemists) and asked what they thought it could be. They said I should see a doctor immediately. They gave me directions to the nearest clinic. I rode the trolley a couple of miles and it dropped me off at the doorstep. Mind you, it was Sunday evening. I went inside and there were a couple of people waiting. They took my information and charged me the holiday rate to see the doctor- 55 dollars Australian which is about 40 dollars US. I sat in the waiting room and before I could even start reading one of the magazines they called my name. The doctor looked at it and said it was cellulitis, an infection of the skin. She prescribed a strong antibiotic and sent me to the pharmacy. There I handed in my prescription and they filled it in seconds, not like the States where you drop it off and maybe you can pick it up in an hour if it's ready. But the biggest difference was the price. 15 dollars Australian (that's about 11 dollars US). Not only did I get great health care but at a reasonable price.

IT JUST DOESN'T GET ANY BETTA

The name of the clinic is Betta Health, no lie, that is the correct spelling, and they told me to come back in two days. I went back after taking antibiotics orally for 24 hours with no results. In fact, my arm was getting bigger. This time the clinic was very busy and I had to wait about two hours to see a doctor. This new doctor was not happy with the prior treatment and said I needed to go to "casualty" (the emergency room at the local hospital). I rode the local tram to the Royal Melbourne Hospital. There was the usual line that emergency rooms have, but no problem being seen without insurance. They just took my address in the US and promised to bill me. No Worries.

The casualty doctor said we should do I-V antibiotics. They injected the new medicine in my hand and explained that it would run up through the arm - which felt better immediately and the swelling went down right away. He said I should come back the next day and get another shot and to stop taking the pills.

When I awoke the next morning the arm felt much betta and the swelling was way down. First thing in the morning I went to the Melbourne Aquarium. It was very impressive. I got there during feeding time and they had two divers go into the tank and feed the rays, turtles and sharks by hand, in order to keep the fish from getting all the food. Some of the rays were over five feet wide and they still had their stingers on. It was very interesting and the turtles were biting at anything and everything.

It was around noon, time to go back to the hospital. My arm was beginning to throb again and I decided to take the tram. On the way to the hospital yesterday I noticed several bike shops. I decided I would take some literature for Baker Drivetrain and Indian Larry Legacy and drop it off. The first shop was a Harley Davidson dealership. They wouldn't even give me the time of day. I may be on the other side of the world, but some things never change.

The next shop I went to was H.D. Development. It was a really old-school shop with mostly pans and knuckles. They were purists in there, the bikes were all bobbers and choppers and they only use original Harley motors and parts.

I spoke to them about the Baker six-speed and they replied they had no use for it- that 4 gears were plenty. I almost totally dismissed these guys because I have a knuckle and I know that it needs at least one more gear if not two. I went outside and smoked a cigar and tried to regroup. After returning and making small talk I got a tour of the shop. Upstairs there were five complete engines, two Knuckles and three Pans, all complete. In another area they had eight or nine more complete motors. Again, Knuckles, Pans and generator-Shovels (I did see one Evo, but I think it was there by mistake). I asked if they were for sale and he said, no way. They were going to build bikes around those engines. Downstairs was much of the same. It was a really cool shop. It was like going back in time. Back in the '70's and early '80's if you went into an aftermarket shop and started asking questions the owners would tend to be a little unsociable. Well this is a step back in time.

When I checked in at the ER it was a whole different experience - after all I hadn't been there for 24 hours. Now everyone got a wristband with their name and stats on it. The woman told me NO worries while I was waiting in line to register. The man behind me was holding his chest in pain and I could see his shirt come out with every heart beat. I decided to let him go in front of me and check in first. When the receptionist finally got finished playing with her computer she looked up and asked what was the problem. She said he looked fine and "no worries." I am getting way over this no worries stuff.

After another couple of hours a new doctor saw me. He began a whole new diagnosis and treatment. I explained what I was told the day before and together we came to a compromise with the treatment. They gave me another injection of I-V antibiotics and told me to start taking the pills again. The official term for my condition was "olecranon bursitis" which was causing "cellulitis." Well at least this takes my mind off my missing motorcycle.

Awwww this brings me to my motorcycle. I received a call in my motel room from the DMV. They needed a copy of the invoice for my motorcycle. I explained that I had the title and registration, but they wanted a receipt from when I bought in 1997. Of course I had no such thing so I had to fax them a letter saying I had no such thing. Its getting old, but at least I feel like I'm heading in the right direction. My broker called and said once this clears the bike should be released the same day or the next. I kinda think this is wishful thinking, but at this point I need a little hope.

A DINGO ATE MY BABY

Well the swelling went down in my arm and the numbness went away with it. In its place is the pain. I feel like it's a step in the right direction though and hopefully it will be behind me soon.

I called the state about my bike and was given the largest runaround speak yet. Basically I should be happy that it is not going to take the required 17 day application time. He couldn't tell me when I would get the bike, but not 17 days. I have had about all I can take at this point. Every ounce of me wants to show these Australians what "going postal" means. To top off being stuck here in Melbourne for almost a week and a half, they are having the G20 Summit meetings here this weekend. The already crowded town is now getting way overboard. I can't take much more.

I decided I needed to get away. Fast and far. I booked a flight to Alice Springs which is in the center of the country. There I reserved a rental car with all the camping equipment included and headed to the outback. I will be visiting the famous Ayers Rock (where a dingo ate my baby- you know the movie), Olgas, Kings Canyon and just take in a little nothingness. I feel better already just getting away from everything.

I am hoping when I come back my bike will be ready and I can ride away. Until then, "I'm worried."

HOME ON THE RANGE

First, I want to thank everyone for their thoughts and concerns about my elbow. It truly helped a bad situation seem a lot better. My elbow is almost completely better now, however I think it will have a sore spot for a while. Nothing that will keep me from riding though.

What is keeping me from riding is the equivalent of our DMV in the States. I won't take our DMV for granted any more. It may take all day standing in line but I have never heard of anyone anywhere taking 17 days to review an application that I didn't even know I needed. I am hoping when I return to Melbourne tomorrow night I will have the bike.

When I got to Alice Springs, which is in the center of Australia, I rented a car, a station wagon, that came complete with camping gear. I didn't want to rent a bike because after all I could have done that to begin with and saved a whole lot of money. I will wait to ride my bike. The car has everything including a gas stove, water, dishes, even table and chairs. I needed a lot of supplies and I knew I would be far from anything resembling civilization.

I drove about 400 miles my first day into the outback. I ended up at Ayers Rock also known as Ulura to the Aborigines. I had to drive through about five towns on the map. When I got to them they all looked the same - one building that serves as the store, gas station, pub and who knows what else.

Ayers Rock with the neighboring Olgas is a great site. I hiked around and took photos, but it was a bit touristy. I camped at their park and all the campers had to get on one little spot of well manicured grass, not my idea of camping. It was late so I had no choice.

My first meal there was some Kangaroo fillets that I bought. They were only about 6 dollars a pound. They were incredible. I am a steak eater, but I think Kangaroo is even better. When the meal was over and the sun went down I slept 'till dawn.

The next morning I got up and wandered around for a while. I thought the outback would be all dessert but I found that there is plenty of vegetation growing out there and a lot of color. The sand and soil are a bright red color so the area looks like Mars. The morning was cool as was the night, but by 8:00 AM you can feel the heat moving in. I went back to the car and started the drive to my next stops which are all the way back toward Alice Springs.

I stopped on the way at a camel farm. There are many camels in Australia. Back in the 1800s the Australians brought Afghanis over with their camels to transport goods through the outback to Alice Springs. That was about a two week trip, one-way. In 1929 the railroad was completed - they named the train the Ghani. Now the Australians had no use for the camels so they told the Afghanis to shoot all their camels and go home. The Afghanis pretended to shoot them and actually drove them into the dessert instead. Today there are over 400,000 in the wild. I learned that and a lot more at the camel farm. I took a short ride on one but didn't have time for a two-day safari which would have been cool. I saw they also had camel burgers on the menu. I think I'll stick to my Kangaroo.

I continued on, but now it was starting to get late. I tried to get into the first canyon, but it was closed so I found a dirt road a little farther along, drove down that track and hid the car like I do my bike, out of sight so there will be "no worries." I cooked up the last of my kangaroo with a pound of fresh Australian prawns. A little surf and turf. It was dark now and a zillion stars were out, like sleeping in a planetarium. If there were any animals around I'm sure my snoring kept them away. The short tour of central Australia was great, but pretty soon I was back in the city hoping to pick up my motorcycle.

LET THE RIDE BEGIN!

Well today was the day. I couldn't believe it would really happen, but it did. I finally got my bike. I went to the brokers' warehouse and rode with them to DHL with the stack of paperwork. Which left me with only had one more hurdle to jump. I owed the "storage fee" for my motorcycle because it wasn't picked up immediately. They calculate the fee by the weight and the measurements of the container. Well the crate was huge and it was very heavy. The total calculated was $3,200.00, but that was in Australian dollars. They agreed that was insane since the shipping fee itself was 3200 dollars (US) so they let me have it for 300 dollars, I can handle that. I probably would pay anything at this point. I just want to ride my motorcycle.

We hauled the motorcycle back to my broker's warehouse and began uncrating it. Before I left Miami I had Louis and B.K. at Lost Beach Cycle help me tighten everything up – before that the bike would leak all over the place. Amazingly enough my bike sat in that crate for almost a month and there wasn't even a drop of oil under it. And, it fired right up. My battery is a couple of years old now, the Harley Gods are smiling down on me.

Steve and Dennis at Advanced Logistics in Melbourne are the people that made it happen. They don't have a web site yet, but if someone was ever going to ship a bike over or anything else for that matter, contacting them before hand would eliminate all the hassles that I went through.

I only had fumes in my gas tank, but it was enough to get me to the gas station. I don't know how many liters are in a gallon, but my tank was empty and it holds five gallons. I filled it up for a mere 25.00 dollars (that would be about $20 US). The best thing about that though is that regular over here is 91 octane. I put in premium though (cause that's how I roll) which is 98 octane. My bike loves that stuff!

I got onto the freeway and practiced riding on the wrong side of the road and passing on the right. I had to get the hang of it quick. When I got back into Melbourne city center I exited and was now learning how to ride in traffic. Bikes are allowed to cut traffic (split the lanes). Every road in the city is shared by electric trams that ride both ways down the center. There are also more people on the sidewalks than you see on a busy day in New York City and they are crossing everywhere. Melbourne has signs that say right turn from left lane only so not only do you have to yield to pedestrians, oncoming traffic and two way trams but now cars and trucks coming in your same directions. Sometimes it is just easier to say three lefts make a right.

I got to my motel, threw the bags on the bike and was gone in a minute. You would have thought I owed them money I left so fast! - I was ready to get on the road.

I got on the Princess Highway and headed south to Geelong. From there I got off and rode to the Great Ocean Highway. It is a lot like A1A along the coast, but the coast down here has mountainous roads overhanging the beaches. The road will wind back and forth up and over the hills and then back down to the beach, this pattern repeats over and over. As I was riding over one hill high above the ocean there were a bunch of overhanging trees above the road. I saw people pulled over and when I looked up there was this fat little Koala Bear sleeping in a tree above me as I rode under. I had to turn around and check that out again. It was just too cool! I have been taking a lot of pictures on this road and will have them posted as soon as I can. I finish the ride on Great Ocean Road tomorrow (which will included riding by the 12 Apostles). Then I have to make a beeline back to Melbourne and catch an evening ferry ride to Tasmania.

TASMANIAN DEVIL

I finished riding along the Great Ocean Road, the 12 Apostles are really cool. These are rock formations that stand on the beach in the surf. Several of them have been demolished by storms so there are only seven left. This ruined my hopes that I could be the thirteenth, but maybe that would have triggered the apocalypse. I found a shortcut back to Melbourne and arrived an hour before it was time to leave on the ferry. It's called the Spirit of Tasmania. After security went through my bike and bags I was allowed on the ferry. I had a room with a window (It's a 12 hour ride so a bed is a big plus). The ferry left at 8:00 P.M. and arrived at 7:00 A.M. They had a great restaurant so I had a Tasmanian seafood dish. Good choice. I went back to the cabin and laid down when the ship started rocking and rolling. At times it felt like I was moving up and down about 10 feet (kind of like sleeping on a roller coaster.) I must have been tired because I was out like a light.

In the morning I went down to the garage and prepared to leave. I was talking to several of the other bikers and discovered a couple of different bike parties and shows. I now had a destination, so upon exiting I headed straight for Lacerton. I was looking for a bike party hosted by the local chapter of the Rebels M/C. I was having trouble locating the party – I wasn't lost though - when I stumbled upon Richardson's H.D. It's a great shop with a museum and very friendly staff. They work on any Harley including Iron-head Sportsters, which hardly anyone will touch these days. I had a great time there, but needed to head over to the bike show.

I was only a short way from the Rebels clubhouse and when I got there they started tripping on my bike. There aren't a lot of chopped Road Kings over here and they wanted me to enter it in their show. I usually don't, but decided to anyway. After the judging was announced they called my name for first place. Now I knew I wasn't going to win for best of show or best custom, but I wasn't ready for Best Rat Bike. Well I know my bike is different and it isn't everyone's cup of tea so I was just as honored because in my eye, it's the best ever for what I do which is ride and then ride some more. I am racking up quite a lot of miles and many experiences and tales. Now that I think about it that's what a rat bike is so I'll take that trophy.

After the show I rode to a small town called Cambels town. The sidewalk that ran through the town had a single row of bricks all the way through from one end to the other. In the 'States people can buy personalized bricks as a way to raise money for charity or building projects. Well these bricks had the names, dates and origin of the prisoners that were sent here and also listed their crimes. Australia was used as a prison by the British from the 1700's 'till the 1800's. It was real cool to read all the bricks. The crimes were great. One guy got life for uttering fraud. Uttering fraud? Today he would have been a great politician!

RIDING BITCH IS NO FUN!

I got up around 7:00 A.M., jumped on the bike right away and began rolling through small towns on the way to Ross, which was holding an antique bike show. After finding a cafe with latte (every town has a cafe and a pub) I made the short ride down to Ross. They had so many cool bikes there. The earliest bikes were from the 1910's, and they had them all the way up to the present although the majority were British bikes from the 1940s and 1950s. There were Indian Fours and Arial Square Fours, Vincent Black Shadows and many others that I have only seen in books. It was really cool, but I must admit it leaves me wanting more than the several I already have.

At the show I bumped into a friend I've been corresponding with over the internet. His name is Robyn and he's from Hobart. He welcomed me and said if I wanted to ride south he and his friends were leaving at 1:00 P.M. I was about 15 minutes late leaving and they were already gone so I went blazing through the hills and "twisties" (turns). I was dragging the floorboards constantly, and dodging the wallabies crossing the roads, and finally caught up with them after about 60 kilometers. We enjoyed some lattes and a couple of meat pies at a local café in Swansea. I decided to head north up to Coles Bay, and they went south to Hobart. We agreed to meet the next day at Joe's Garage, a local hangout for bikers.

The ride to Coles Bay was nice but I thought Coles would be larger. It was very small and the choices for accommodations were limited. I had my choice of backpackers inns (hostels), bed and breakfasts or a couple of swanky resorts. OK, it's been awhile so I opted for a resort. This place was right on the bay with a glass wall that looked out at the bay. Ultra modern, it even had heated floors throughout (the carpeted living and bedrooms and the tiled bathroom). The wallabies came up to the rear glass doors all day and night begging for food. I had to feed them. As friendly as they were I don't think I was their first. I couple of them even had their young along, with their heads sticking out of the pouches.

As always I got up early and everything was closed. Finally I rode back to Swansea, only an hour away, and found a café. Nothing like pancakes with fresh banana and syrup topped with vanilla ice-cream. After that great breakfast I rode south along the coast taking in the breathtaking views and tiny little towns scattered along the way. I found a remote beach (Roaring Beach) in a small town called Nubeena. The sand dunes were about 50 feet high around it and the waves looked so inviting. If I had a board I think I would have stayed there for a couple of weeks. It was a true hideaway. I was looking for Brooke Shield because it did look like Blue Lagoon.

I rode as far south as I could and now had to turn around and back track to get back to Hobart. On the way I hit reserve so I began looking for a gas station. I rode forever with nothing in sight and as I was climbing a huge hill I ran out completely. I pulled over, got off and leaned the bike all the way over on the side allowing the few remaining drops to spill from one side of the tank to the other. This got the bike started and up to the top of the mountain before running out, and now I could coast down. I coasted a couple of Kilometers, but after a few close calls with passing cars and a logging truck I decided to pull over and wait for some help. Just then a Harley rolled past and I waved. He waved and went past. I realized I should have done something besides wave since he probably thought I was being friendly. Well I am new at this, but he must have known I had a problem because after a few minutes I heard him coming back. John said the gas station wasn't far and he'd give me a ride. I haven't ridden on the back of a bike in way too many years, but I was happy to ride with John and come back with the gas I needed. Thanks John - I'll buy ya a beer at Joe's Garage Tuesday.

BRAKES ARE FOR SISSIES

After getting my gas and getting back on the road I headed into Hobart. It was getting late and chilly and I was tired, but I wanted to find Joe's Garage first. I had been talking to Joe via the Internet and he had seen my V-Twin TV episode and wanted me to stop by. I had already met up with several of his patrons in the time I've been here and wanted to see this hangout. When I finally arrived, Matt, the actual owner, was very hospitable and invited me back the next night for a party.

The morning came and I decided to go for a ride. I did a scenic loop south of Hobart. It was all coastline and really nice. I left all my luggage at the motel so I had room on the bike to relax and enjoy the ride. I felt like I had only been riding an hour or two when I realized it was around 5:00 P.M. already and I needed to get back to Hobart. I washed my bike at my motel and rode over to Joe's. He had me bring my bike inside and park it on the floor. Up on the walls he had several TVs on, all of them playing my V-Twin DVD while the people rolled in. It was pretty cool talking to everyone and answering all their questions. Before I knew it was 11:00 P.M. Having missed dinner Matt offered to cook something up. I am not a big chicken eater but he made me up a chicken burger that was out of this world. Many thanks to everyone and I hope our paths cross again.

The next morning I got up early and started riding across the southwest coast to Queenstown. The ride was about 120 miles but it was through a rain forest and very high elevations that reminded me of the Continental Divide. The narrow road was nothing but curves and more curves back and forth up and down. Seldom did I every get over 45 miles an hour.

Around one particular curve I was heading a little bit too fast and dragging my floorboards when I hit a bump and totally bottomed out. It was a scary sound, but I thought everything was alright until I applied the rear brake at the next corner and discovered there was no rear brake. I was heading downhill at the time and gaining speed on the wet surface. When I hit the front brake the wheel locked up. Knowing that if I leaned over for the curve the bike would come out from under me, I kept going straight. I got stopped but had to cross the on-coming lanes to do it. If another car had been coming I would have been toast. When I pulled over to assess the situation it turned out the steel brake line had been pinched shut between the frame and the road. I tried squeezing it with pliers to open it up but had no luck. I was going to have to finish riding all the way to Queenstown, through the mountains on mostly wet asphalt, with only front brakes.

There weren't any bike shops or even auto parts stores in Queenstown, just one auto-repair garage. The guy there said I had to go to Burnie, about 135 miles away. It looked like it was going to rain all day but halfway to Bernie it started to let up, and that's when I came to the road construction. They had a couple of miles of road torn up, the surface was dirt and they'd been using a water truck to keep the dust down. With the rain the whole thing turned to mud. Having no front fender I was slinging mud everywhere and couldn't even think about using my front brake. I got through and had to pull over and clean my windshield so I could see. I didn't make it another two miles before hitting another construction zone. Man this was getting old. I arrived in Burnie at dusk covered in mud, tired from the day's ride and ready to sleep.

First thing in the morning I rode to a brake and clutch repair shop. I removed the line and took it in, they cut out the smashed parts and spliced in a new piece. The whole thing was a breeze to put back together. Then all I had to do was fill the reservoir and bleed the brakes.

GOODBYE TASMANIA

It was a short ride to Davenport where my ferry was leaving at 8:00 P.M. I got there early and had time to kill. I thought I'd have a burger for lunch. This was the first time I had a hamburger here other then McDonald's. I asked the lady for a cheeseburger with no onions or tomatoes. She said a cheeseburger only has cheese and nothing else. A hamburger has everything including cheese. Ok, then I said, "Give me a hamburger with everything but onions and tomatoes." When my burger came I had to inspect it to see what all the stuff on there was. It had a fried egg on the top, some sort of meat patty (reminded me of my Marine Corp days) with lettuce, beets and pineapple. I was hungry and I ate it, after pulling off the beets, but I think I'll stick to McDonald's in the future.

Next, I stopped at an Internet cafe to use a computer. There are many places here where a person can get on-line, the cost is about three dollars for a half an hour. There is a big difference though in the speed of the computers. Some are way too slow and make it almost impossible to email pictures to my website. I just so happened to be visiting one of those shops. It took 10 minutes just to log on so I tried to log off to leave and that took another 10 minutes. As long as I was waiting I went up to the counter to order a vanilla milk shake. The man asked me if I wanted ice cream with that. I said if it didn't have ice cream it would just be a glass of milk. He looked at me like I was from Mars so I dropped it from there and just asked for a milk shake with ice cream.

I was out in the parking lot with still another four hours to kill when a young guy came up and started talking about my bike. He said he worked at a bike shop nearby. When I found out they worked primarily on Harleys I asked for directions to check this place out. I was parking in front of the shop and two of the guys walked out to check my bike. They invited me in and I met more people and the owner.

Next thing you know work came to a standstill and we sat around for a couple of hours and talked motorcycles. Here I am on the other side of the world, but it's all the same. The shop was called Speedway Road Motorcycles (speedwayroadmcycles@big-pond.com). I got the full VIP tour. They had complete rooms full of vintage stuff. I remember 25 years ago shops in the States used to have all that stuff, but its all been sold over the years and now it's hard to find. A lot of it probably ended in shops like this one far from home. I'm glad the people who have the stuff appreciate it like we used to.

Before I knew it, it was time to get to the ferry for the ride back to Melbourne. I said goodbye and we all took pictures of each other and I rode off. I should have stuck around and tried to barter some parts off of them, but I'd probably just end up moving there, settling down and that would be the end of my world tour. They did give me a T shirt that I will wear with pride.

Once on the ferry I couldn't get a reservation at the nice restaurant, they wanted me to eat in the cafeteria. I charmed the girl at the door and an hour later I was eating fillet mignon. "Life is good" was the last thing I remember thinking as I fell asleep in my cabin an hour later.

MELBOURNE TO SYDNEY

I had a few days before I had to be in Sydney and although I could have made the ride up from Melbourne in one day I decided to take the long way and head up the coast, taking my time and seeing the sights. I thought the road would run entirely along the coast, but it jogged back and forth so the views of the coast itself were limited, unlike the Tasmanian coast. The weather was also cooler than I planned, it seems the forecast means nothing. Many times it looked like rain, but I only got caught in it once.

My first stop was Lakes Entrance. It's right along the coast on the north end of 99 Mile Beach. This town, like all the towns on this part of the coast, was very small. There isn't too much to these towns except a few small motels, some restaurants, a gift shop; and every town has a pub most of which are also casinos.

The next day I rode on to Eden. I had a banana milk shake there. Yes, I got a glass of milk with a banana in it. I have to remember to ask for ice cream in my milk shakes next time, I'm learning. A lemonade is a sprite soda. Takeaway is what we call carry out. Sausages here are like our hotdogs and that is their good sausages. I have had some that tasted exactly like Vienna sausages - I don't order sausages any more. I order over-easy eggs every morning and get something different every time, from over-hard to poached. I was in a grocery store and noticed that even their carts here are different. Have you ever gotten a cart with a broken wheel and it pushes crooked. Well here they have carts where all four wheels swivel like the front wheels on our carts. Now everyone in the store is pushing carts that are out of control. It is hilarious to watch people trying to turn corners. It's these little differences that make you realize you are somewhere other than home.

I spent the next night in Norna, a bigger town, but it was Sunday and everything was closed. I hadn't found an Internet place in two days and was having withdrawal. The owner of the motel gave me a few ideas about where to eat, but most of those turned out to be closed. I called one that was open and only a few blocks away. I jumped on my bike and half way there got stopped in a DUI roadblock. I pulled up and before I could put the kick stand down the officer had a hand held thing, the size of a big cell phone, stuck up in my face and told me to count to 10. It seems here they don't need probable cause or your consent. I don't drink or that would have been a major problem. He decided to check all my paperwork, the Florida registration that I had in my wallet was expired, the current registration was with all my other paperwork that I handed in to get my permits. He lectured me about keeping everything with me at all times. I agreed and apologized, and didn't get deported.

The next day I finally arrived in Sydney. I was here a day early to meet my friend, Tattoo John from Ft. Collins, Colorado. Everything was looking good except that I had another medical issue. One tooth had been bothering me for a while and in the past couple of days it suddenly became a lot worse so I made an appointment for the next day with a dentist there.

STUCK IN SYDNEY

I made my dental appointment from an ad in the phone book. It turns out the dentist was a woman. Staring at her sure beats staring at the ceiling. The painful tooth had a cracked filling, I thought it was the one next door with the chipped crown. Man, I need health insurance, but the gypsy biker union I belong to doesn't have any. She did an X-ray and then filled both teeth for a grand total of 400 dollars. That was far less than I expected which meant I would not have to worry about what I could eat.

I was ready now to meet my friend John at my motel the next day. When he was several hours late I began to wonder. I started thinking; Australia is across the international date line so when he said the 6th in Tahiti, where he was living in a hut at some tropical island paradise, he meant the 7th in Australia. That evening he emailed me and affirmed what I thought, but in the morning he emailed again that he missed his flight. It was time for a change of plans.

I was staying at the Travelodge in Sydney. It was 110 dollars a night, but I also had to pay 20 dollars a day to park my bike – which was a deal because it was locked up and under guard. Harleys are a big theft item here. When I tried to book the room for two more nights they raised the price to 145 dollars per night. Now I am getting way over my budget. I started shopping around, checking out the many "backpackers" hostels. Most of these are dorm rooms you share with strangers which I didn't like in the Marines and don't like now, but they're only 30 dollars a night.

I went across the street to a pub that had rooms and the woman there had a room for the second night but not the first, at 110 per night. I checked out of the Travelodge and went back to the pub. Now she said there was an opening for the first night too. I was trying to be cheap so I told her I would spend the first night at the hostel. She told me she'd call and book me in another hostel because the one I was talking about had bedbugs. I reconsidered this whole cheap plan of mine and immediately booked the room for both nights. She liked bikes and as we talked she reduced the rates for me and got me tickets to keep the bike parked where it was. Sometimes no plans work out the best. I had extra time so I went and bought Christmas cards. I took them to the park, and filled them out while I smoked a cigar.

LEARN TO SPEAK LIKE CROCODILE DUNDEE

After getting my Christmas cards mailed out I decided to ride around and check out some local bike shops. I stopped at a nearby shop and got directions to their main shop in Parramatta, a nearby town. I ventured out with what sounded like simple directions and ended up riding in circles. When I pulled over and looked in my saddle bags for my maps I discovered that all I had was my US atlas, my Australia maps were in my motel room. Traffic was bad and the bike was hot and after asking several people for directions I was still lost. I kept passing the airport (the only landmark that I recognized) and knew I wasn't figuring out this town. I couldn't even find a gas station where I could ask directions. Desperate, I stopped at a real estate office and asked the receptionist where Parramatta was. She looked the city up in her local atlas and gave me directions. Several other workers there joined in with more and more details. She then photo copied the map and gave it to me. I looked at it and said that I thought Parramatta was a larger road and she said I had asked for Parramalla. I jokingly laughed and said "you say tomato and I say tomoto."

The boss of the office, the only man there, didn't see the humor in this and immediately began demanding reports and told every-one else to get into his office for a meeting. I remembered how it can be a drag to work a nine-to-five job. Meanwhile a customer there knew exactly what I meant and gave me simple directions. I almost rode straight there accept for one wrong turn and I found myself on a freeway going under the Sydney Harbor. It was a long tunnel that went far underground (and water) then back out. It re-minded me of the tunnels in New York City only without the tun-nel bunnies.

I finally made it to The Motorcycle Accessories Supermarket. They had everything from dirt bike stuff to Custom Harley parts. They had a leather OCC jacket for only 800 dollars. It seems that their TV programming is about a year or two behind the U.S. and they have only heard of OCC and West Coast Choppers. Another item I saw on the shelves was a 1% patch. For only $8.95 you can buy one and sew it on your vest.

By this time I had burned up most of the day riding so I began heading back with my original directions, which took me straight back into the city. Of course it helped when I got close enough to see the sky scrapers.

Back in Sydney I found my new favorite Greek restaurant and had my usual, roast lamb with potatoes, or was that potatoes. Afterwards, I smoked a Bean're Select. I have been smoking so many Cuban cigars that I was missing my own. I went back to my new motel room and tried to go to sleep, but all I could hear was the live band playing in the pub downstairs. They quit at 2:00 A.M. so it wasn't too bad. I should have been down there anyways. As has been said, "if it is too loud, you are too old."

PIRATES OF THE AUSTRALIA

I got up early in the morning as usual. John was supposed to be arriving at 8:45 A.M., but I hadn't heard from him in a couple of days. After my morning coffee I sat at a sidewalk cafe table across the street from my old hotel to wait for John. I had moved from the Travelodge, but that was the place where I told him to meet me. I thought he would be a little late, but by 11:00 A.M. I was beginning to doubt that he made his flight. I walked down to the internet cafe several blocks away and started updating my web site. After about an hour I got an email from John, he was at the Travelodge looking for me. I told him to stay put and I went back and met up with him. We had lunch at one of my favorite places while John read my blogs about how hamburgers are prepared. But like me, he had to learn for himself. When he got his burger with an egg, pineapple and beets I laughed. He pulled them off and ate it down swearing never to order that again.

I thought he would want to wind down and take it easy from the long flight, but he was full of energy and wanting to get on with the trip. I told him I had contacted a Harley rental shop, Rolling Thunder (www.rollingthunder.com.au). We decided to jump on a train and try to find this place. It was easy riding the train to the suburb, but once we got there we were lost. I found another real estate office and they gave directions and a map. After a short walk and we were there.

Maurice, the owner, was not expecting us. He said we were lucky the bike was in, but it needed to be serviced before going out. I thought this would just be checking the oil and gasoline but they did a thorough inspection and decided to put a new front tire on it even though I thought it was fine. This was going to take a little time. Maurice said to relax and if we wanted to stick around, he was having a BBQ and party in the afternoon. I decided I needed my bike so I left John and rode the train back to Sydney, got my bike and returned. On the way back the beautiful sky turned cloudy and overcast.

The party had already began when I got to the shop. John and I ate and smoked some cigars and did the VIP tourist thing, answered questions about the US, and took pictures. One of the guys at the party said he had seen John and I walking down the street earlier and thought we looked like two pirates. It was dark now and a lot of people were beginning to leave as the weather was really looking bad. When it began raining both John and I realized we'd left our rain suits at the motel, so we decided to hang.

I talked the mechanics there, Dude and Biff, into changing the oil for me. While they were working on that I got them to fix an exhaust leak that I had too. We hung around the shop working and talking while the party continued up front and made plans to go out on the town the next night.

By the time they finished the work on my bike it was past midnight, but the party was going strong so we hung around some more. The rain continued all night so we just hung around till dawn. They definitely know how to have a good time here. We barely made it back to the motel before checkout time. There was no time left to shower, but the girls at the desk told us to take our time and check out when we were ready. The plan was to stick around for another day, but John was ready to go so rather than try and find another room we loaded up our things and rode out of town, heading north on the Pacific Highway. Sorry Dudes, we'll have to catch a rain check on the after-hours tour.

It was Saturday and a lot of places were closed along the way. We had difficulty finding somewhere to eat and as the evening approached we pulled into Newcastle, hoping to find a room. We had trouble finding a motel and rode back and forth, but every motel we found had the no-vacancy sign out. One had a vacancy sign up, but when we went inside they said they just sold that last room. I told John it was because we looked like pirates.

We found a tattoo shop and John got them to help us out. They looked in a phone book, made some calls, and booked us a room. After thanking them we rode over, checked in and found a pizza joint right down the street. We ordered the pizza take away but when it was ready we sat at a table to eat it. When we were done John asked for some napkins. And then they instructed us that to eat take away in the restaurant was illegal. We can break the law with out even trying.

It was dark now and with limited sleep the night before we retired early and prepared for the next day's adventure.

EVEN THE BEST FALL DOWN SOMETIMES

When the sun came up I was ready to ride. I had been in Australia for over a month and taken my time seeing all the sights along the way. I now wanted to ride as fast as possible and get to the gold coast where the scenery changes and the Great Barrier Reef begins. John however, had different plans. He hadn't seen anything so he wanted to stop and check anything that might be of interest, which included several rides back to the ocean and then turning around and having to back track. We did find a national motorcycle museum, which had over 700 motorcycles. I liked that, they had a lot of cool parts I would have liked to bring back to the states, but they wouldn't sell anything.

We didn't make it far before the day was over and we got a motel in a small town. We went out for dinner, but the whole town was closed and deserted. We found one restaurant open. I wanted to park in the front so I could see the bikes so we parked in a no parking zone. The street was empty except for our bikes. Inside they said they were closing but we could have 15 minutes to eat if we hurried. We ordered and it came in less the 5 minutes. We were wolfing our food down when in walked two police officers. They hung out at the front and just waited. I hadn't seen any police anywhere all day and now they just happened to show up. We were paying for our meal and they made small talk with us. They asked if we were on motorbikes then asked if we were going to keep riding or stay? We told them we had a room and were leaving in the morning. They seemed relieved and away we went.

The next day we got up early again. John wanted to visit an old prison he heard about and we rode off to find it without my morning coffee. There were no signs and it was off the highway quite a bit. We kept getting turned around and then while I was trying to make a u-turn in the street I rode up a median, bottomed the frame out and with my front wheel dangling about six inches off the ground I fell over. I got off and picked up the bike, but it was stuck on the median and wasn't moving. Meanwhile John was busy trying to take pictures of my situation. He finally put the camera down and gave me a hand - and never let me forget it the rest of the day.

We saw more sights including a bluff overlooking the surf. It was cool and we took some great pictures. Then we climbed down onto the rocks, they were like old lava formations, and walked around while the waves crashing over. It was nice. We found some deep pools of water that had filled during high tide. By the time we found them the water was warm from the sun. One pool was the size of a big Jacuzzi and about eight feet deep. We jumped in and it was great. While I was in a decided to soap up and wash my hair. There's just something great about bathing outdoors with sunglasses on. It was really refreshing.

We rode on but it was starting to get late. We stopped in a little town where I found a thrift store. I bought a blanket for four dollars and a sheet for three. I was ready to camp. John had his camping gear on the bike, but lost his sleeping bag somewhere, so he went back and bought another blanket.

I wanted to find a place by the beach to camp. We rode up the coast and found a cool place, but it was in a small town and had a lot of No Camping signs. I stopped a little farther along and parked so I could walk along a sandy trail I found. I thought maybe we could ride the bikes down the trail and hide them and camp there out of sight. As I'm walking down the trail John blazed by me and made it about 20 feet before the bike buried itself in the soft sand and over he went. I had my sweet revenge. Karma. He didn't bust my chops any more for falling over.

After all that I didn't like the stop so we rode on. It was dark now and I saw a big kangaroo bolt across the road. I knew it was time to stop so we pulled over and camped in the woods instead of on the beach. We smoked a cigar then John was out first leaving me trying to doze off while laying in the dark listening to the kangaroos rustling in the woods. They sure make a lot of noise as they hop around. Some ax murderer would have made less noise navigating through the brush.

SURFS UP!

We awoke at sunrise, loaded up the bikes and rode north. Within a few miles we came across a herd of Kangaroos lounging in a field. We pulled over to take pics and they all bolted in every direction but ours. There were even more then we originally thought, but they all ran.

Back on the road we made a few stops in sleepy little coastal towns. In one town I found a cool pair of white sunglasses. I bought them and now I really stuck out. I rode with them on and we were drawing a lot of attention. I thought they looked good, but I am not sure that everyone agreed. I am an American and that's my freedom of choice.

We heard a lot about Surfers Paradise. When we got there it was like Myrtle Beach, very touristy with skyscrapers all along the beach. It seemed like a great place to stay so we got a nice two bedroom apartment with great views so I could watch the surf. Pretty soon I had to get out there so I hired (rented) a surfboard for 24 hours. This would give me plenty of time to hone my skills and become a professional surfer. I paddled and fell and fell and paddled. I would go out and the waves would push me back in. Once, while paddling out, a wave picked me up and I was riding it backwards until it sent me down and tumbled over me. Throughout the day I give it my all. And all I ended up with was a giant rash, it looked like carpet burns, across my chest from lying on the board and paddling.

When the sun started to go down I finally quit and went back to the room to clean up so John and I could go out for the evening. It was a pretty young crowd, the drinking age is 18 and most of the people looked to be under 21. We walked around and around and thought maybe it would get better as it got later so back to the room we went to wait. After a little TV we both passed out, missing whatever the night had in store for us.

I got up at dawn ready to do this surfing thing. I went in the water and immediately the salt water burned my red chest. Lying on the board was almost unbearable. I tried to ignore the pain and paddled out. It was close, I almost caught a few. Once, I was able to get up on my hands and knees before the tip of the board dug under, sending me flipping and twirling under the water. I went back in to the beach and let John use the board. He agreed, the surfer thing is a lot harder than it looks.

By now it was time to ride anyways, so I brought the board back to the rental spot. We checked out of the room, started riding north and ended up in Brisbane in no time. It is a very large city so we decided to try out city life for a change. We kept getting lost (which happens when you have no destination) and traffic was bad. We couldn't find any motels and when we did they were all booked up due to a two-day Robbie Williams concert. I had never heard of him but a lot of people apparently had. We finally gave up and decided to get back on the road and just ride.

THE LONE RIDER

We were riding north in the afternoon. We hadn't gotten very far when we saw a sign for Glasshouse Mountain. John had read something about it so we detoured to check it out. It wasn't too far and had some great views. The day had evaporated and it was already 4:00 P.M. We stopped at the Wanderer, an open-air cafe. We were trying to make plans on where to go. I pulled out my map. It was a motorcycle map with stories of the 100 top rides in all Australia complete with pictures. I was reading a story when I saw the picture of the very same cafe where we were sitting. We didn't need the map at all.

We found a campground next. John didn't want to sleep in a spot where we could get in trouble, like the side of the road. We found a nice legal campsite with great views, but it was getting dark and it wasn't long before we were out cold.

I got up first the next day and rode into the nearest little town, Melany, to have my coffee and use their internet. John road up shortly and we thought we'd try and find the metal sculpture shop we saw in this brochure that he had. We rode past it the first time then circled back and found the shop, but it didn't open till 10:00 A.M. Earlier I saw a sign for some falls so we doubled back and checked them out. They had a swing rope about 20 feet above a pool of water. You could swing out and drop or opt to just dive off the falls into the deep water below. John did both first while I was getting ready. We swam around for a while, but pretty soon I was ready to get back on the road. We'd been in this same area for way too long and I really wanted to put in a day or two of nothing but riding so that I could make it to the northern tip of Australia. John wasn't interested in going north so we agreed to split up.

I wanted to check out a beach I heard about on my way north, Noosa Heads. It was a beautiful beach that reminded me of the Virgin Islands with its houses built right into the hillsides, and overhanging bluffs with crystal blue waters below. There weren't many people there either and I thought about camping, but there were a few more hours left to ride so away I went.

The road felt good under me. I usually travel alone so this was a very comfortable feeling. I made some good time and was ahead of my schedule. I rode through Gympie, some locals told me there were a lot of inbred people here. As I rode through I thought that it was quite possible so I kept right on riding. I was making great time, but hadn't eaten and so I pulled off the highway in a small town called Tiarro.

I thought the town had a restaurant, but it only had a pub with a restaurant. As I pulled up there were a lot of locals hanging outside - there is no smoking inside anywhere in Australia. They were all looking at me and talking to each other then laughing, and then looking and talking and so on and so on. I went inside and this place reminded me so much of the bar in Crocodile Dundee that it wasn't even funny (maybe I was in Walkabout Creek). Inside I found that I had to wait until 5:00 P.M. before they started serving dinner. I waited the 45 minutes and then ordered. I was OK with everything until some of the local girls started checking me out. I know from experience that if there is one thing that gets a redneck up and at it, it's when their local girls start paying attention to an outsider. I ordered a steak and veggies and when I got my order the veggies turned out to be sliced whole pumpkin which tasted like sweet potatoes. I ate quickly, happy to ride off. When I looked in my mirror everyone was still standing on the sidewalk.

I kept riding into the dark. I was worried about kangaroos, but what was worse was all the road train traffic. A road train is a tractor-trailer pulling several full sized trailers. I was sandwiched in the middle of a convoy of these and it was quite nerve racking. They like riding way too close for me which kept me close to the truck in front of me. As I'm riding in the middle of my lane I saw a dead kangaroo in the middle of my lane and had no time to dodge it so I hit it and went airborne. I landed safely but the trucks cattle-guard was only about 20 feet behind me ready to plow me under the next time.

I pulled over to get fuel and regroup. When I tried to pay for my fuel with my credit card there was a problem again. It seems that Bank of America put a hold on everything. I had emailed them earlier notifying them that I was in Australia, but they felt I needed to call. This was a major pain and I decided to deal with it in the morning.

Not far ahead I found a rest stop but it seems here you are allowed to camp at rest areas. I pulled over, rolled out the blanket and listened to the birds doing their jungle sounds and watching the many shooting stars as I drifted off to a much-needed sleep.

THE JOURNEY CONTINUES ON PAGE 241

chael Lichter

USA MADE **RENEGADE WHEELS**
Custom Motorcycle Wheels

Paul McKelvey

Michael Lichter

Michael Lichter

Michael Lichter

© G. Russel Childress www.maineventimaging.com

233

Jack Mcintyre

BAKER

BEER SECURITY GUY

235

BLING'S CYCLE "IRON CROSSES ARE CLEVER BUT DIAMONDS ARE POWERFUL"

TEN PART 2

AUSTRALIAN TOUR
THE JOURNEY CONTINUED FROM PAGE 224

I fought the law but the law won.

Sleeping on the ground was getting a little old. I didn't have an air mattress and the ground was quite hard. I was up at dawn ready to make an early start and put some miles down. I had 1000 miles to go to get to Cairns, one of the most northern towns and fairly close to the Great Barrier Reef. I wanted to go diving at the reef, and figured the farther north I could get, the shorter the boat ride to the reef would be.

After rolling up my bedroll and strapping it on the bike I hit the highway. There were no towns or houses or anything along this stretch, just softly winding highway with very little traffic. The road was feeling good and I was rolling a little fast and the next thing I knew there was a cop coming in the opposite direction.

The speed limit is in kilometers per hour and my speedometer is in miles per hour, but that didn't matter since just after I arrived my speedometer broke. I'd been guesstimating my speed, but I wasn't doing a very good job of that.

The cop car had his lights on before he even passed me. I knew he had me so I pulled over fast hoping he wouldn't notice that my brake light stopped working. As he was parked and getting out of his car I slipped my half shell helmet off, hung it on the handlebars and stood up. He asked for my license and I thought I would be off the hook since I had a Florida license. He had already observed the Florida plate and wanted to know why I was going so fast. I couldn't tell him I didn't know how fast I was going so I just said something like, "ahhh I don't know." He said he clocked me doing 130 kph and the speed limit was 100kph. Now I thought that sounded pretty close but apparently they are very strict, even five-over is too much. He went back to the car, got his ticket book out and started writing.

Next he came back and wanted to know why I didn't have my helmet strapped on. I showed him that the strap had broken (another thing I have been meaning to fix) and was held together with a zip tie. I can just pull the strap over my chin when I'm putting it on. Taking it off I just pull the helmet down over my face and it comes off instantly. I demonstrated this and he didn't like that at all. He said it was plastic. I knew I was in trouble when he wanted to see it - inside it had a sticker that said "this helmet is for novelty purposes only and not intended to be a safety device." Again, he went back to his car and started rearranging things in his back seat. I thought for sure I was going for a ride. Instead, he came back with a camera and started taking pictures (maybe he has a web site too). He then wanted to know where my indicators (turn signals) were. Before I could say anything stupid he interrupted and said this could go on all day. He gave me a 150 dollar ticket for speeding and a 225 dollar ticket for no helmet (guess they have no ticket for novelty helmet). I thanked him for cutting me a break and rode off.

This really bummed me out for the day even though I should have known better. Bike laws are strict over here and most riders wear full-face helmets and almost everyone wears a motorcycle jacket even in 100 degree heat. Also, I still needed to deal with my credit card problem, which added to the stress.

An hour later I found a town and got online and tried to settle the dispute with Bank of America. After that failed I had to buy a phone card to call long distance to the credit card company. After being put on hold several times they told me that they were just helping protect me. When I explained that I emailed them three times and that they have no toll free number for outside of the

United States they really didn't care. It was like, now I was inconveniencing them. That was Bank of America if you were wondering who not to use.

While in that town, still fuming from the ticket and the credit card issues, I found a camping store. I went in to get a pad and all they had were swags (they are a mattress-sleeping bag combination that is very comfortable but very large). The man kept trying to sell me this thing for 185 dollars. I told him I was on a bike and he showed me one with a "bikie swag" sticker on it. It was the same size. I decided to continue roughing it and left.

I rode 'till I needed gas again, and found a thrift shop right nearby. They didn't have much, but low and behold they did have a rolled up pad for camping. The price was just five dollars so I didn't even try and talk her down. Total in camping gear is now just 12 dollars. Sweet.

I got back on the road again and kept going till I needed gas. I needed to make time, but it was so hot out it was tough to keep going. All I could think was to turn around and go back. Everyone has been telling me how hot it is up north but I really wanted to see the area. It was a long day and when it was over I made it to Mackay, about 500 miles.

I got a room, showered and went out into the setting sun to look for dinner. There were thousands of birds flying around and chirping like crazy. I have heard of this before and at first didn't think anything about it, but when I looked up I saw they were all parrots and parakeets of every color in the rainbow. I had to stop and stare up at the sky as they were flying around. The locals all had this look like it was no big thing. I walked on and found a great Thai restaurant. After some spicy pad Thai I was back to my air-conditioned room snoring and content.

I don't even think it was dawn before I woke up. Those same birds that I thought were cool the night before were out again raising cain. I felt like telling the locals that not only was this no big deal, its was a bit of an inconvenience. None the less, it got me up and rolling. I wanted to make it to Cairns.

A good night's sleep really did the trick. I felt great and never even thought about the day before. The heat I was dreading towards the middle of the day didn't come. I hadn't realized that a lot of the coast runs through rain forests. These are almost chilly even in the middle of the day. I passed some really cool things, making plans to stop on my way back south. Tully, which has class 4 whitewater rafting on a section with over 22 rapids, was one of the spots I promised myself I would check out on the way south.

I made it to Cairns well before dark. I had been putting on sunscreen over the past weeks but my face was still burned, maybe that's why riders here where full-face helmets. I found a room and before having dinner and retiring, I made a reservation to go on an all day dive trip to the Great Barrier Reef the following morning.

THE GREAT BARRIER HURLE

I slept great and woke up early as usual. I needed to be at the downtown harbor at 7:30 A.M. The woman at the desk said it was only a short walk to the harbor and that I should leave my bike. Walking would leave the bike in a more secure parking area, but everyone in Australia always says, "It's a short walk," and five miles later you are still not there. I started my walk and in a half an hour I was almost there, and I walk fast. I found a McDonalds on the way. They open earlier than anyone, so I got my favorite McLatte. Next to that was a juice bar and I had a large fresh drink made with carrot and pineapple juice. I was trying to be healthy since I was going diving all day and would be out at sea far from any McDonalds or anything else for that matter.

I got to the dock and saw the boat. It was a large high-speed cat with air conditioned cabins and seats like an aircraft. By 8:00 A.M. we were on our way. On the boat I learned that the Great Barrier Reef is over 1000 miles long and has over 2000 named reef formations. It took us an hour and a half to get to our first destination. There were beginner divers and snorkelers and they got to walk down the steps at the rear of the boat and into the water. The certified divers like myself got to take a step off the side and drop about eight feet into the water. With all our gear on I felt like Jacques Cousteau.

I was alone and you must have a buddy to dive with so they paired me up with two girls. The three of us were in the water and ready to descend. I let my air out of my BC but stayed on top. I swam back to the rear of the boat, got another weight and swam back up front and the three of us tried again but still couldn't so I swam to the rear again and got yet another weight (this made six). I was finally ably to descend, but barely. From all this swimming forwards and backwards I was huffing and puffing pretty good and never really caught my breath before I went under so the entire dive I was going through some air. I was the first one finished and had to surface with only a minimum of air left.

The Reef was incredible. I read somewhere that the reefs in the Florida Keys are very comparable to the Great Barrier Reef and that if you've done the Keys it's a very similar experience. Having done both now, I thought this was totally different. The reef went down 60 feet with many overhanging parts above your head and I saw several tunnels a daring person could swim through. I was very impressed with the reef and the aquatic life and could not wait to dive again.

As soon as we were back on the boat they had us take a 10 minute break and then begin suiting us up for the next dive. The boat attendants said that my wet suit was very buoyant so they gave me a heavier air tank and seven weights. That makes that eight foot plunge quite thrilling wondering if you are going to come back up to the top, but I did not have a problem. I felt really good and so the three of us descended at once and I had no problem. We swam the opposite way this time and it was amazing how big this reef, one of over 2000, was.

Along the way a large flat fish, almost the size of a manhole cover, swam around each one of us getting close enough we could touch him. After that he started returning to each one of us again. He just couldn't stop checking us out. He finally swam away. It was very cool. I stayed down almost twice as long as the first dive. We finally had to surface and we all came up together. The minute I surfaced I took the regulator out of my mouth and burped. Well without getting too graphic I got to see that large fresh juice I had for breakfast. I was feeling fine up until that point, but after that I hurled again. This was obviously not the way to impress the ladies so I let them swim ahead and when we reached the boat they didn't even know I had gotten sick. I am smooth. On the boat I was still feeling a little queasy, but they were serving lunch. I was really hungry at this point and even though I was a little scared I did eat lunch. Then I ate seconds then even went back for a third sandwich. They had fresh pineapple and I ate that too.

We were going to move the boat to the next spot and after about 15 minutes of setting the anchor they said we were there. I didn't even know we left. Apparently they only moved the boat a short distance. Everyone began suiting up for our final dive. I decided to take this one off and chill on the boat. I was feeling good and I didn't want to do anything to change that.

There was a cricket game on the television, but cricket is always on the television. Members of the crew were constantly coming in to check on the score and then going back to work. I talked to the captain and learned some facts: A cricket game lasts about five days playing eight hours a day with an hour break in between. People call in sick for a week so they can watch the game. All the wives in the 'States should be happy, their husbands only spend Sunday afternoon watching sports. I could see someone in the

'States telling their wife, "Honey I'm going down to the bar to watch the game," and not returning for five days.

Once everyone finished the dive we took several headcounts to make sure we hadn't left anyone before heading back to port. From the ocean view I could see how the rainforest in the hill came right up to the shoreline all up and down the coast of Cairns. It looked just like a very large island in the Caribbean and the water was just as clear and blue.

I said goodbye to everyone and went back to the motel. I was worn out and wanted to eat dinner and go to sleep. My plan was to get up early and head south to Tully where I would spend the day white water rafting. At dinner though I met someone from Papua New Guinea who encouraged me to talk to some of the diplomats that he knew and possibly go over to his island country. To do this I had to put off leaving first thing in the morning. I thought I should do this because I had nothing to lose and the next morning I went to meet them. They weren't all in the office, but I gave them my pitch and was told I would be notified through email. I was hopeful, but being a realist decided to start heading south to Tully even though I would be too late to raft on that day I could spend the night at nearby Mission Beach. I had my new camping pad I wanted to check out. I was heading for my next adventure and open to any possibilities.

WET DREAMS

It was a beautiful day riding south. I wasn't going far, only about 50 miles. I wanted to keep riding and take advantage of the great weather, but had to stop in Tully where they had the white water rafting business on the Tully River.

I arrived about 3:00 P.M. The trips leave around 8:30 A.M. so I made arrangements to go out the next morning and then rode over to Mission Beach, a small town about 15 miles away. I thought that the name Mission Beach sounded familiar, but I still don't know why. It is a very small town on the coast. It was a town stuck in time, very laid back, no one was in a hurry. I have a little bit of a hard time relaxing and am always on the go, but for some reason I was ready to chill in this town. It had a bunch of internet cafes so I was able to tend to my web site and get caught up. Then I went and looked for a place to camp. I wanted to stay right on the beach and found a campground that was owned by the city. They were keeping it all natural and primitive which is more to my liking. The campground was right on the beach, the office was just a little camper with a tarp for a patio. I asked about a camp spot and the guy there said it was 12 dollars a night. I gave him a 50 but he didn't have change. I explained that I was going out to dinner, and he said for me to just bring the money later and he would hold the spot right on the beach for me.

I rode down the beach road to find a place that had been recommended to me for the best roo (kangaroo). It was Scotty's. They served the roo in a plum sauce and it was excellent. It was dark now and I went back to my camp ground, paid the manager and set up camp. I laid back on my bedroll and smoked a cigar thinking about life as I looked up at the zillion stars. It was a surreal feeling, like there wasn't anything else that mattered in the whole world. I felt like nothing could touch me if I just stayed there forever. I drifted to sleep, but sometime in the middle of the night it started to rain. I gathered up my stuff and carried it over to a pavilion then I went back for my bike. I was raining heavier now. I parked the bike under the small pavilion, laid out my bedroll on a picnic table and slept the rest of the night there.

DELIVERANCE WITHOUT BURT REYNOLDS

The picnic table I slept on was not the most comfortable even with my foam camping mattress. Needless to say I got up early, but I also needed to so that I could have my morning latte and a light breakfast. I have learned to check out the local merchants and find out who opens earliest in the morning before I go to bed at night. That way I always get my coffee.

Having had my latte and pancakes it was now time to start
making my way back to the rafting company in Tully. This was
about an 18 mile ride from Mission Beach. Mission Beach is in a
Cassowary preserve. A Cassowary is like an ostrich but with a
very colorful blue and red head. They have talons on their feet that
can be dangerous. I didn't see any at the campground, I was hoping to see some on my early morning ride, but no such luck. It was
very overcast and several times I would pass sections of the road
that were wet from the rain. Without a front fender, that's all it
takes to get me soaked.

I pulled into White Water Extreme right on time. The tour bus
coming from Cairns was late though. There were about 65 people
going out with us today. The people already there, myself included,
were loaded on the short bus and taken up the river. I guess I'm
just a short bus kinda guy. Along the way we were given an educa-
tional speech about the rules of rafting then we were divided up
into groups of five and six. There were several groups of three on
board so they paired them up which only left me. I was told on the
larger bus there were five Swedish female volleyball players that I
would raft with. When we got up river the larger bus was waiting
and the rafters were standing by their rafts. When I got to mine I
was paired with a family from England – mother, father, teenage
boy and girl; and a German guy of questionable sexual orientation.
But then again with my white rock star sunglasses they were probably wondering about me too. Not my ideal rafting group. I was
ready to raft though and decided to make the best of it. Once at
the raft I jumped in first wanting the best seat up front. The
teenage boy was next to me with the females in the rear.

Our guide was a cool guy - I think that is a requirement for
river guides. I told him there would be a tip for him if I came out
of the raft. This is not the thing to say if you want to stay in the
raft. On our first set of rapids he spun the raft around backwards
at the last second and we went through in reverse. I couldn't see
behind me and totally lost my bearings and next thing I knew I
was flying through the air. I was hoping the raft was under me

when I landed, but when I hit the water the heavy current sucked me under even with my life jacket on. I knew I'd missed the boat. There were guides along the banks and on the rocks throwing ropes to me in case I was in trouble, but I swam to the raft and they pulled me in before the next set of rapids. As it turned out, the boy was tossed overboard too. Now we were having some fun.

Farther down the river there were some serious class-four rapids. Several people have drowned in this section so the rafts went slow, one at a time, with the other rafts parked along the banks and "spotting" for one another. This was definitely the safest way, but I wanted extreme. There may have been some drowning before, but not today, I'm pretty sure there were none the day before. I always say you have to break a few eggs to make an omelet.

We got thought those rapids intact and I was really excited about what was up and coming. There were about 20 more sets of rapids with some great sounding names - sharks tooth, zig zag, etc. – ahead of us. As the day went on the rapids got smaller, however. The best ones were at the beginning.

We stopped for lunch and I thought that was going to be a big feast, but it was only a burger and bug juice (fruit punch like kool-aide). I seemed to be the only one paddling and when I'd turn around to check I was confirmed of this. The mother said it was a woman's prerogative not to paddle and being a good daughter, the girl followed her mother's beliefs. The trip was a work out for me.

At the end we carried our rafts back up the hill to the trailers and loaded them up. We then went in the changing rooms, got into dry clothes and went to our busses. We all went back to the rafting company headquarters where the cafe turned into a pub. While everyone ate and drank, the employees were busy selling pictures and videos and T shirts and anything else. I hung around for a little, but decided to make haste.

I loaded up my bike and rode south. I only had a few hours of riding left in the day, but I made it to Townsville that evening.

Having ridden through Townsville on the way up it was like being in a familiar town back home. I knew where all the motels were and even the internet cafes. I found a bike shop and went in and talked bikes with the owner. It really is like being in the 70's here.

In the morning I got up and needed to put a few miles down. I wanted to make Brisbane. I thought it was about 1000 kilometers, but I was mistaken. It was 1363 kilometers, about 800 miles. I ended up riding into the night, but I made it. This was my longest day of riding yet. I was sore, but it felt good making some time. I still had about 1500 miles to go and I couldn't be late.

TIMING IS EVERYTHING

I rode like the wind and two days later I was in Brisbane. Even in the seedy part of town they wanted 100 a night for a motel room. I talked them down to 80 which I felt was a rip off, but when I went into my room it was the nicest room of my whole trip. It came with free secured parking, free internet and the rooms had everything including flat screen TVs.

I would have never guessed it, but I felt bad checking in late which meant I would only have the room for 12 hours. So I immediately booked it for another night. The next day I just chilled, watching TV, ordering room service and going downstairs to use the internet. This turned out to be a good plan since the weather really turned bad. It rained most of the day so I didn't feel bad about laying over an extra day.

I emailed John and said I would meet him in Sydney the next day. I had about a 600 mile day ahead of me so I checked out and rode away well rested. I was making good time, but as evening approached the weather moved in. I barely found a motel about 200 miles outside of Sydney before the bottom fell out. I was lucky to find a room just in time, it rained off and on all night.

In the morning I packed up the bike and before I finished a light rain started to fall. I put on my rain suit and took off. It was very overcast but didn't rain. I knew better than to take off my rain suit or it would have begun again. About 50 miles outside of Sydney it started raining again and kept going until I got to the city. I pulled up by my old motel and there was John, it was good to see a familiar face.

I checked in, got cleaned up and we headed out. We did all the tourist stuff. We went through all the parks and worked our way down to the Sydney Opera House at the Harbor. We people watched most of the day then had dinner and went out on the town. The nightlife here is different than in the states. We found some bars with live music, but they were playing 80's dance music. I wasn't too fond of that in the 80's and It wasn't growing on me now. We made the best of it and ended staying out most of the night.

The next morning was Christmas. Everything was closed. I was in my motel room and it was sad not doing the traditional thing with family and friends. Being a gypsy is my life and most of the time I love it. This was not one of those times. Times like this make me analyze what my life is all about. By the end of the day I realized that I can't always have everything I want. This is the trip of a lifetime and the timing was right for a trip of this magnitude. No matter how much I wanted to be somewhere else for Christmas, I couldn't trade that for all the good experiences I've had on this trip. The memories will stay with me forever, kind of like tattoos.

I contacted the airlines about maybe changing my ticket and heading into Asia before returning to Miami, but they wanted 4000 dollars for a ticket. I didn't ask if that was US dollars or Australian. Either way it was way too much. Vietnam would have to wait another day. Besides, I would need weeks to do Asia the way I want. I will get there one day when the timing is right. After all, timing is everything.

I'M OVER CRICKET

I stayed in Sydney too long. I wanted to get back into Melbourne to make sure I had plenty of time before leaving. It is only about a 600 mile ride, but I didn't want any surprises. I needed to get to the shipper's office. These guys had my crate, the same people who helped me so much in getting the bike accepted in the first place, Advanced Logistics.

On the ride back to Melbourne I wanted to stop and visit some friends in Canberra, the capital, but it wasn't on the route I took. I started on the M5, shortly after Sydney and it changed to the M43 then A43 then some other road then to the Tullamarine Highway. Every time it changed I'd have to pull over and check the map. I had forgotten my atlas in my motel room in Sydney. I could have forgotten something more important so it was no big deal. Highways in Australia never have north or south on them, only city names, and if you are not sure where the city is it can be hard to navigate. Especially when they name the smaller ones instead of the larger ones you're more likely to recognize.

About halfway back I was reflecting on a couple of things I didn't get to do. One was a visit with some friends at Phil's Garage, a motorcycle shop. I wasn't sure where it was, but as I was thinking this, riding though a small town call Albury, I looked over and there was the shop. It was like I saw the promised land. I pulled over and wouldn't you know it, they had taken two weeks off for the Christmas and New Year's holidays. I left a note and some goodies, T shirts and stickers, and found my first internet cafe since leaving Sydney.

I checked my emails and looked at the clock. I needed to make a decision. Should I stop for the night or keep going to Melbourne. It was 3:45 P.M. and I was still three to four hours from Melbourne. I decided to keep going. It was a nice warm day and I had plenty of daylight left. I took off and about an hour or two away from Melbourne it started getting colder and overcast. By the time I was almost into the city I stopped again to put on a coat and gloves. I was happy to be pulling into familiar territory and went straight to my favorite hotel, The Victorian. Once inside I was informed that they were all booked up. It seems the Ashes, the super bowl of cricket, was in town!

After searching several motels I was told I'd have to go outside of Melbourne to find a room. It was late, and I was cold and tired. I found one room but they wanted 400 dollars. I couldn't live with myself if I spent that much on a room, unless I had some one to share it with. I'd left all my camping gear back in Sydney because I thought I was through camping. If I stayed in Melbourne I would have to sleep with the street people. Riding back out of town I stopped at one last place and they had one room left. It was about 11.00 P.M. now, I was grateful and I took the room.

In the morning I rode out to meet the broker. This was same guy who picked up the bike from the shipper when it arrived in Australia. He gladly took the bike from me, had it crated and shipped by boat back to the states. This cost about half as much as shipping by air, but takes several weeks at a minimum. Then I went straight to the airport and just hung out waiting for my flight that evening. Due to the fact that Australia is separated from the US by many time zones, I was able to see the sun come up twice while in the air getting home, first between Australia and L.A, and then again on the flight from L.A. to Miami. The long flight didn't stop me from going out once I arrived home in Miami for New Years Eve. The end of the Australian adventure was just like most of the events in my life.

One adventure doesn't really end. It seems more like the end of one becomes the beginning of the next and the two kind of blend together to become one continuous adventure.

WOLFGANG PUBLICATIONS

✪ ✪ ✪

ILLUSTRATED HISTORY
Sturgis 70th Anniversary $27.95

BIKER BASICS
Custom Bike Building Basics $24.95
Sheet Metal Fabrication $24.95
Sportster/Buell Engine Hop-Up Guide $24.95

HOT ROD BASICS
Hot Rod Wiring $27.95
How to Chop Tops $24.95

MOTORCYCLE RESTORATION SERIES
Triumph Restoration - Unit 650cc $29.95
Triumph MC Restoration Pre-Unit $29.95
Harley-Davidson Panhead Restoration $34.95

CUSTOM BUILDER SERIES
How to Build an Old Skool Bobber Second Edition $27.95
How To Build The Ultimate V-Twin Motorcycle $24.95
Advanced Custom Motorcycle Assembly & Fabrication $27.95
Advanced Custom Motorcycle Chassis $27.95
How to Build a Cheap Chopper $27.95
How to Build a Chopper $27.95

SHEET METAL
Advanced Sheet Metal Fabrication $27.95
Ultimate Sheet Metal Fabrication $24.95
Sheet Metal Bible $29.95

WWW.WOLFPUB.COM

✪ ✪ ✪

COMPOSITE GARAGE
Composite Materials Handbook #1 $27.95
Composite Materials Handbook #2 $27.95
Composite Materials Handbook #3 $27.95

AIR SKOOL SKILLS
Airbrush Bible $29.95

PAINT EXPERT
Kosmoski's New Kustom Painting Secrets $27.95
Advanced Custom Motorcycle Painting $27.95
Pro Pinstripe Techniques $27.95

TATTOO U Series
Into The Skin $34.95
Tattoo Sketch Book $32.95
American Tattoos $27.95
Body Painting $27.95
Tattoo - From Idea to Ink $27.95
Tattoos Behind the Needle $27.95
Advanced Tattoo Art $27.95
Tattoo Bible Book One $27.95
Tattoo Bible Book Two $27.95

NOTEWORTHY
Guitar Building Basics
  Acoustic Assembly at Home $27.95